Other books by the same author:

THE SECRETS OF ALEISTER CROWLEY
THE RIDDLES OF ALEISTER CROWLEY

The Wrath
of
Aleister Crowley

by
Amado Crowley

Diamond Books

Published by Diamond Books, Morrison Stoneham, Prudential Buildings, Epsom Road, Guildford, Surrey

First edition 1994

Any and all correspondence intended for the author should be directed to: BM–Box 77, London, WC1N 3XX, without the author's name. Please include an International Reply Paid Coupon, but please note that the publisher cannot guarantee a reply.

I dedicate this book to all past Members and Officers
of that glorious example of living occultism:
Ordo Templi Orientis.

I merely wish that there were many more of them.

Contents

Preface

This is the third book that I have written around my father's life and his special brand of occultism. The first was 'The Secrets of Aleister Crowley', (1991). The second was 'The Riddles of Aleister Crowley', (1992). And now this: 'The Wrath of Aleister Crowley', (1993). If I don't watch out I'll be a success.

Time is passing. I'm getting older. But I'm not a morbid man. Since no one in my family has yet slipped me a surgical catalogue, I assume I am still working well. There is no shake in my hands. My dentures are not stapled in. I can still reach the toilet in time. On the whole, I'd say I was wearing quite well. Even so, I am wearing. I get aches where I never used to. If I see a five-pound note, I put my foot on it. Then, twenty minutes later, I have to ask someone help me lift it off. My knees, you see, are not so pliant. It's like the mountains really ... going down is easy. It's getting up that's bad.

If people see you kneeling, either they think you're having a quick pray, or that you're dossing down for the night. I once sat on the steps of a church, and a robust Christian lady thrust a bowl of soup up my nose. It was tomato. Very red. I thought she was about to bite my neck, so I stabbed her with my cane. She was well protected by layers of faith and thick flannel. She wrenched the cane out of my hands and wrung its neck. "You're a dirty old man," she accused. "If you sleep by the river, I hope it floods!" She snatched back the soup-bowl but, sadly, not the soup. When I got to my hotel, they thought I'd had a haemorrhage.

The worst is my skin! I used to have such fine features. As a teenager, when most boys are saving up for plastic surgery, the girls said it was as soft as a baby's bottom. My skin, that is. Now it is more like wrapping paper that has been saved from last Christmas. Or it could be my eyes. I suffer from presbyopia. No, this doesn't mean I'm psychic – you can't buy glasses for that! It just means I have very long sight. I have to cross the street to read a newspaper, so to speak. Millions have the same defect. But I'm the only one who buys a ticket for the cinema and goes into the non-smoking section of the usherette's blouse.

The mirror does not lie. I see the reflection of someone I don't remember having met. The whole of life takes on the air of a shop window display. Gradually, I am joining the past. The only consolation is that so is the O.T.O. and the Golden Dawn. At an age when I should be saintly, I enjoy being impish. No, I am not more evil – just a wee bit bolder. I have had to develop new, facial expressions. 'Angelic' when they look at me, 'horrified' when they look at someone else. It may all have to do with 'The Kama Sutra', which is not the clearest book in the world. I took it that 'sixty-nine' was the age at which one started. I still limp in cold weather.

Do you believe in fairy stories? 'Sleeping Beauty' is a simple tale which veils a secret truth. Forget what they said about her pricking her finger with a spindle! Ignore the athletic Prince who leaps over thickets to kiss her coma better. He woke her, that's all that matters. To be quite honest, I suspect he would probably wake me! You don't often see a Royal Highness strutting about like a coat-hanger. Not unless you play polo. Her name, by the way, was Aurora. This means Dawn. It was after her radiance that 'The Hermetic Order' was named, though they may not know that.

There you are! You thought I was joking. Well, perhaps I was, but even humour is a way of telling you something. Why should I be as dry as a Sunday sermon? I don't accept that a laugh or a smile can ruin the truth. It's a shame they don't laugh more at the United Nations. As for any animosity toward me or my father – it's nothing compared with all-out, bloody war.

Why do Occultists think that 'serious' means 'solemn'? Why do they treat AC like Hamlet when he played the role of Bottom? Pope John-Paul I was one of God's Clowns, and they killed him. Rasputin was also a bit like that, and they killed him too. Persons of great dignity see something dangerous in men who see truth and still laugh.

It's a pity that no individual nor any organization has sought to have charge of *The Book of Desolation*. But I have done what Aleister told me to do. My conscience is clear. All they had to do was tap me on the elbow, and ask a polite question. They scoff instead. They call it a cock-and-bull story. But the point is, they never even asked to see the book or a photocopy. So why then do they condemn it? Perhaps they appreciate its importance, but do not know how to get their hands on it? What they say, of course, is: 'We didn't want the idiotic book anyway.' Do you believe that?

I assume I shall have to publish it myself. One must be wary with assumptions though. Even the Virgin Mary made do with one. You see, I don't want to force the burden on others. It's not what AC would want. The book is best written[1] by me because I knew him and I'm in tune with his way of thinking. There is just one small problem: I neither wish to make money, nor lose it. But a book of this kind would have a very small public. Therefore, it must carry quite a high price. Perhaps we shall need to make it a subscription edition.

Meanwhile, this present book puts the accent a little bit more on Aleister's thoughts and teachings, as they were shared with me. You will see that I do not haul down the magical traditions. If you pay close attention, you might even see *A Door*. If this should occur, it is your own affair whether to go through or not. It won't be automatic in any case. You would need to prepare. But if you see the truth, it will give new meaning to everything!

---

1. It has already been translated. It exists in a form of archaic English. If I were to publish it, as it now exists, it would simply read like a Lutheran version of a mediaeval Highway Code.

1

BAPHOMET

A figure standing for Behemoth[2] and, hence, one of the secret symbols for God

Learning

People think they are studying 'Occultism'. They are actually reading 'history'. But it doesn't upset them. They don't worry because they're not aware of their mistake. They are engaged in a superior pastime, so they don't complain. They'd think twice if they knew where it was taking them. But even when they count the cost, they won't like to admit that they were cheated.

They feel quite chirpy at the outset. It is all hot and highly relevant. They learn the jargon to start with, then a new system of thought. It looks occult. It smells occult. What more could they want? They forget that 'being interested' is not quite the same thing as 'finding truth'. I'm so sorry. But we do not get the measure of paradise by the strength of our emotions. Take lust for example. Then take 'Madonna'. You must see what I mean.

If you apply the same rule to occultism, most people seem ever so happy just to be paddling in 'ancient secrets'. All they are actually looking for is to have their emotions moved. They go by their feelings, not by reason, so all they ask is "impress me". In this spirit they swallow stuff that looks as though it was swept up in Berwick Street market! On a barrow-boy's stall, they give it a grin. From a 'guru's hand' they take it like babes. They like a secret language too. They like to bandy about 'in' words like Cabala, Golden Dawn, Pagan and Vibes.

They are sitting ducks. They are easy targets. So like mindless sheep, they follow the first shepherd who wanders past. Or the

---

2. Originally given as the hippopotamus, and a beast of the Jewish apocalypse, (cf. The Book of Job, 40).

1

Pied Piper of Hamelin. He soon gets them 'high' on something 'new', and they are ready to die for him. Indeed, they have been dying in large numbers for many years. Perhaps this is what they mean by "an encounter with God"? Once they are committed they find it hard to say what they are committed to. It is a kind of dream, I suppose. But unlike many other dreams, this one is impossible. They laugh like men. They behave like men. But they are no better than dummies which are wearing souls you can hire.

"It's called sociology,[3]" AC said. "Making wooden models of airplanes does not really qualify one as a pilot. Cutting hair does not make you a brain surgeon. So what good does it do, to pray to the Sphinx? It will get you where it got the Pharaohs, I shouldn't wonder. Dead!"

You know why there's a lot of interest in the ideas of ancient Egypt, don't you? As AC said, it's because they're dead! Their amazing religion got them flattened by Roman boots. Rome won. Do you know of any occultist who looks at Roman magic, or speaks the Etruscan language? It's not exotic enough! It does not fill the bill!

You may take the wrong path. But it's like taking the wrong bus. You can't just change. You have committed yourself. You bragged too loudly and too long. It would be hard to take all their giggles and snide remarks. You have wasted so many years. But you prefer to waste more rather than admit it. So when you speak now, there is no conviction in your voice. It has been replaced by vehemence. What you lack in truth, you try to make up for with zealotry. But this is how we become fanatics – by never questioning our own opinions.

Brave New World
Take 'New Age' magic, for example. One hopes that the people who go in for it are sincere. They are entitled to do their own thing and spend their lives as they wish. But on what grounds do they assume that the Gods agree? I accept that they are not fond of authority – yet they abrogate the Gods' authority to themselves. What if the mystic salad won't do? What if they can't stand the spiritual hot-pot? What if the Gods prefer men to have 'will' and not to display their lack of it?

3. "A man-made concept which the faithful defend to the death but which has no useful application."

2

One advantage with New Age magic is, you needn't know a thing. And so it follows that you can manage without formal education and even intelligence. Please note: I am not saying that New Age followers haven't got them. I'm pointing out that they are surplus to requirements. You can do fine without. You can look like a hedgehog, and pick up ideas along the way. This is free-flow, spiritual freedom. You can mix African and Afghan. You can be a pacifist who knocks hell out of all who disagree. You can even take ruinous drugs and try some Holy Healing. Crazy man! It is the first religion that ever welcomed parrots – and social anarchy.

The Tarot is nice. Crystals are cute. The same goes for runes and incense and bric-a-brac from India. Is this the great secret? They know all about that on Ward Twelve. Don't they know about synergy? Don't they know that you can mix things together and let loose a hidden power? Take a schoolboy example – some sulphur, a bit of charcoal, and the nitre scraped off the walls of a cave. Bang! You've got gunpowder. Great fun, of course. It blew my best friend's eye out.

It isn't easy to put unlucky students back in one piece again. The accident is more often mental than physical. They usually go mad and stay like that for years. Don't mock. Ask a priest. Or ask a doctor. The pathetic fools have their good days now and then. Once a year, they may rise to the surface. They scream out "*J-e-s-u-s!*" and go back down again. One of the cabbages turns its head. "Wow," it says. That is all it has ever said. It is faintly possible that they are enjoying a trip to the astral plane. It may even be 'instant sartori'.[4] But there is no sign of relief, only of pain. This is what divides 'delusion' from 'mystic union'. Some keep, others lose, their contact with reality.

I have sympathy for people who put faith in New Age mysticism. But there is no short-cut. They are not the centre of the cosmos and they are doomed to fail. I do not attack the ones who practise it. I attack the ones who cash-in on the market. The former are not so much 'believers' as 'customers'. The philosophy is aimed at the jobless, the aimless, the rootless, the weird, the way-out, and the great unwashed. It is designed for the fringes of society. It is a talisman dangled in front of the cancer of despair.

4. A state of enlightenment that is the goal of Zen Buddhism.

Carry On Revolting

You are not the sort of people who would interest the Masons, are you? You don't find occult groups queuing up to recruit you? This is odd. Very odd. It is even weird, when you know that one of them is the driving force for the 'New Age'.

Somebody likes to keep their tabs on you! Why? Not to save your souls! You will make very useful fall-guys or scapegoats. In England, when New Age people set off for Stonehenge, the police react with such force, you might think we were being invaded! But you come in very handy as culprits. It's very clever. It flows as smoothly as a well-directed film. It is so ingenious, you will doubt the charges I make. One has got to admire their skill. They use you to play into the hands of the mass media. You are there to shock the country into moving to the Right Wing. But you think you are free.

Your problem is: you don't stop to think. It's what they were counting on. That's how they killed the Cathars and got the Jews. You can't imagine how cunning they are. But by all means, go out and confirm some of the evidence. Why are people so bigoted? Why are mums and dads ready to cheer when 'Law and Order' shoots at you. Don't you see? You are being trained to pull calamity down on your heads – with a little help from your 'friends'.

But to come back to 'serious occultism': its adepts claim to be seeking inner vision, or awareness, but even they look to the past. It's not just Ancient Egypt but India, Tibet, China, Mexico – even Atlantis! These are all spiritual blinkers. It suggests that someone is slipping reins on you, hoping to drive you, and not wanting you to see what you are missing. It is 'mental myopia' and you allow it to happen. You put the blindfold over your 'third eye'. You are on your way to being old and bigoted too. Can't you see the signs?

Work it out for yourself. When the rude awakening comes, will you be ready? When the worst happens, will you keep your mind intact? Then please tell me: where will you find reason, since you haven't got any now? How shall you add one sausage to the sum total of the world's wisdom? And how the hell do you manage to convince yourself that you're okay?

Academic Occultism

If we could pin an expert to cork, like a butterfly, we might dissect him. Then we might find out why he flitters away his one day in the sunlight, nibbling the doctrines of the dead. Those departed geniuses were quite like you. That gives a sort of waxwork feel to magic, and the weird sensation of mummies in the morgue. This may be why so many horror films are inspired by the subject – the 'unknown'.

All experts die in the end. Yet the scope of studies does not grow any larger. Like Shakespeare, Crowley, or Francis Bacon – we get bigger and newer books, but never anything new. It's the same in the field of magic. Scholars know very little more than they did five hundred years ago. As I said, they study history. Only one or two persons a century ever help to make it.

One Freemason says "... there is little doubt in the minds of impartial investigators that Lord Bacon was the legitimate son of Queen Elizabeth and the Earl of Leicester ...".[5] In which case, he should have been King Francis I. But the precise opposite is true. The lineage of Bacon is so clear that no one else has ever thought to question it! But there you are, you see? One makes a little mystery and then one bends it to one's purpose. The Americans call this 'rigging the evidence'. The Americans should know.

Almost every occult order adds fuel to the fire. They do so adore that sense of secrecy. The naive inquirer is urged to search for truth – and they sell him all possible aid, short of practical help. Myth is piled on myth. Assertions are added like arches by architects. The *'Sanctum Sanctorum'*[6] is held together by hope, string and glue. A member may advance in grade. There will be a fee, of course. If he applies himself hard, hard, hard ... he will end up knowing very little about a great many things.

Isn't it strange that we know so little? Oh, a few exalted names have been added to the list. Madame Blavatsky is one that thuds from my mind. Rudolf Steiner is another. Gurdjieff is a third. Not to mention lesser lights, such as Alice Bailey, Dion Fortune, and Israel Regardie. The latter is often called 'the man who changed his mind'. But be honest. Is the world any further for'ard because these folk strolled across the stage? They had their day. They made a living. But most vital of all: they left.

Being 'a good lawyer' means more than passing exams and knowing case law: it means winning cases. Being 'a good doctor'

5. 'The Secret Teachings of All Ages', Manley P.Hall, 1928.
6. Latin: "the holiest of most holy places".

is more than anatomy and pills: it means curing those who are ill. Well, being 'a fine occultist' has nothing to do with books: it means dealing with the Gods and doing successful magic. Yet I hear on the astral grapevine that many scholars have found my books absurd. Since they share the same opinion, they have the same membership card! A perfect explanation of why they did not understand.

They have greater interest in money. Hence they try to make trash of their rivals. Oh dear! It's against the rules. It goes contrary to the oaths you swore to the Gods. Please, don't just take my word for it. Consult AC's old friend, Choronzon. I know him quite well. I'll introduce you, if you like.

"I have done my part in agreeing to meet you," said Aleister to an irksome visitor. "Now let us talk about me. We may be equally vain, but I have the right to be."

Experts

If you're normal then you're putty in the hands of experts. You do not argue with them. You give ground. Aleister said: 'It's easy to test for lies. Believe no one.' But if you read every book on the subject, you would not be an expert. Most of them have been written several times already, often by the same author. It's cold meat warmed up. If we made a list of the world's most pointless books, then occultism would be top – and 'The Guinness Book of Records' would print it. A sad comment on modern values.

There have always been books on taking cars to bits. Now there are sex manuals. It's amazing how all browsers go blind and steer clear of the shelf. I saw an old lady give a quick peep. "How on earth do they expect one to knit that?" she asked the assistant. There are others who wait until they are alone. You can watch them on security video. They happen on the book by chance. They read as keenly as a Finnish dictionary.

It makes one wonder 'what' these authors have been talking about all these thousands of years. As a matter of fact, they've all been giving their own opinions on the same subject. In a certain way, they've all been talking about themselves. Which is, after all, the most riveting topic most people ever come across. It is only one step less than believing that God made creation for you.

Fun-Fair

"Why are you so silly?" Crowley used to ask when a Jehova's Witness called. It wasn't quite such a nuisance in those days. "Come in, come in," he'd say like a gleeful fox welcoming a rabbit. "I'll listen to you if you will listen to me." Then he used their sense of politeness, just as they'd used his. He served tea and cakes while proving he knew the Bible better than they did.

I am not as playful as you might think. I speak from experience. In my career, when I have said something 'new', other scholars snorted: "This does not fit what we know." Well, of course it doesn't. They are expert on what is old. Anything worth saying has already been said – this is how they stand. They said the same thing about Jesus, you recall. But not all knowledge[7] is what we might call 'truth'. That is their big mistake. The normal occult teacher merely tells you what his books say. That is all. He can show you no more. He can not guide you to an encounter with the beyond.

I visit a hospital. I get lost and stumble into the room with the Cobalt Scanner. I am afraid. I do not understand and I feel a faint panic. The nurse tells me its name. I feel better. She tells me what it does. I feel at home. She tells me who invented it and where it was made. I am so relaxed, I could waltz down the corridor with never a care. I do not see the trolley heading for the morgue.

The 'experts' will smile. "Oh yes," they'll nod. "There are people like that." But they never include themselves. They are worse than idiots, who are at least humble. Just listen to them. Do they sound like men who have seen the Absolute?

"If you are looking for a Teacher," said Crowley, "avoid velvet curtains! Only a charlatan sets up a gaudy stall!"

7. Which is often a miscellany of facts picked up from books.

2

URCHIN

The Keeper of Secret Tradition[8]

Therion speaks

AC made an ideal scapegoat. Every group needs one, of course. From village politics and religion all the way down to Occult Orders and drama clubs. They all need someone to blame. Aleister was ideal for the part. He stood out in a crowd. He got up everybody's nose. And he was blunt. Rather like me, in fact.

If you met him, you'd be impressed. He was amusing, charming and, like Byron, dangerous to know. He could delight everyone, much to their surprise. And of course, they fancied they could detect an unknown 'presence' which gave them a rare frisson. It is the feeling one gets in a large museum or an echoing cathedral. The sensation that something is about to happen, and you don't know what. To be honest, one is not expecting that sort of thing to happen at a party. That is possibly why one remembered him.

If Crowley could amuse his friends, he could glue strangers to the spot! He held them like rabbits, paralysed by headlights, and after he had passed, they felt stunned. It made them uneasy too. I'd go so far as to say it unnerved them a little. Never having had such a feeling before, they had to handle it as best they could. *It's why so many decided that Crowley must be evil.*

I was struck by it myself. He seized your attention like your favourite film, and you didn't breathe again till several days later.

---

8. This Great Goddess dates back several millenia. The facts that she came out at night, rolled into a ball, and sucked milk from cows were regarded as 'signs of mystery'. The hedgehog is still regarded with affection today. (cf. 'Gods & Goddesses of Old Europe', Marija Gimbutas, Thames and Hudson 1974.

They say Rudolph Valentino did that to women. They say that Mae West did it to men. In Hollywood, they coined the name 'It'! One has always assumed that 'It' was some kind of instant sex appeal. Some film stars could bring taxis to a halt from one hundred yards. In Aleister's case, it was a magnetic force-field and it did not just come from his eyes. It was there even when he was silent. Laugh, argue, chat about a new play ... he could transfix you like a beetle in a museum of Natural History.

It made one shiver, of course. Afterward, when you began to wonder what the hell had happened, you decided you hadn't liked it. That was mainly because you didn't know what to call it. The experience was so new, so novel, you just couldn't stick a label on it. You had no way to house it neatly among your souvenirs. As a matter of fact, it was precisely this 'unknown' quality that made you react with dread. By contrast, those who knew him well found it soothing to be with him. For instance, he had the ability to help one improve one's astral travel, or take one on a psychic venture. He could embrace you and take your soul elsewhere. The jolt was upsetting to begin with, but one soon got adjusted to it.

What he actually did, of course, was gently to probe your private self. When you realize just how much people hide, you understand why they don't want their minds examined. I can vouch for this myself. He did it to me. When I was seven, I had no secrets so it just felt very peculiar. But when I reached the awkward age, and sex was on the horizon, he made me squirm. When he does it nowadays, and yes, he still examines me, I try to make him chuckle.

It alters nothing at all if you accept my tale or not. The truth is that my friends and I are still visited by Aleister on the astral plane. There you are, you see? That's one of the details that can stagger belief and make your knees buckle. But once you get used to it, it won't frighten you. No harm can come of it. On the contrary, Aleister has been known to do a great deal of good.

Calls from Afar

Usually, or about ninety per cent of the time, I am the one he uses as his instrument. For no apparent reason, the 'bagpipes' start as I begin to wheeze with asthma. I do my best to treat it lightly because other people can panic at what happens. I wish they would remember that asthma is rarely as bad as the symptoms seem to suggest. So the best thing is to keep calm and be normal. This isn't easy when someone is going bright purple and sounding like a Formula One engine about to explode.

Anyway, there I am, chatting away quite naturally, when the lining of my bronchi decides to swell and starts to constrict the tubes. This is not as rude as it sounds. Instead of being able to breathe in and out normally, it is now very hard work. The air fills with the sound of wheezes and whistles, a bit like one of those ancient steam-organs at a fair. People then dash about to find my Ventolin or what I call "my fucking puffer". You can guess how many mistakes *that* has caused! A moment or two later I go quite numb, and up pops AC. He came as a surprise guest in the middle of a recent initiation ritual. After he had gone there was quite a queue for the toilets. The candidate, she was a girl when we started, was quite spaced out – but then she usually is.

He's not the only one, I hasten to add. There are others. Sometimes they put in an appearance before him, with him, or just after. But he usually prefers to do a solo spot, and here there is just one problem. I do really suffer from asthma. So did AC, and still does. So when the symptoms begin, no one is sure whether to get my medicines or fetch a note-book and pencil.

We have talked about it many times. This topic seems to intrigue students far more than things of an occult nature. They must find it a bit more vivid. But here is the vital question: does Aleister trigger my own asthma, or does he somehow inflict his asthma on me? If they happened at the same time, what would be the outcome? Let's hope we can wheeze in the same Key.

You must never imagine that it is somehow 'nice' to be a spirit medium. One gets over the novelty very soon, I can tell you. On a good day, if all goes happily, you don't know anything about what has occurred. They tell you about it later. On a wretched day, if the energies are weak, you have a strange feeling that you might not be returning from beyond. You have a close brush with death.

Imagine how it feels being 'taken over'. There's a stranger in your house, in your heart, in your mind. He has access to your memories and he can touch your personal things – like your fantasies and your internal fears. He tries out your toes. He uses your hands like a pair of gloves. Then it is your tongue. No matter what your own character is, it is put aside. You stop being the person you were. You are erased. You are hauled off stage and someone else takes over. You feel a touch of panic. You woosh along tunnels, through trees, among clouds and, gradually, but quickly in fact, all contact is loosened with the last word you spoke. You are *somewhere else*. You are someone other.

There are many kinds of medium. I am a trance medium. This means that my whole being can be possessed or taken over by another entity. I become 'not me' and, I tell you frankly, it is bloody exhausting. You end up feeling as if you had been mentally and bodily raped. At times I am mindful that one of these beings is peeping in, like indecent eyes at the bathroom window. It is like the 'aura' in epilepsy – it warns of something looming. I smell a strange scent, I hear an inappropriate noise, or I get the feeling of ants crawling over my feet.

But no matter how often it happens, I am never ready. I do not get used to it. I can talk about it now, but it always takes me by surprise. I sniff the air. 'What's that?' I ask. I brush my legs to sweep away flies. I ask if the lid of the freezer is open or has someone just flushed the toilet. I forget that these might be a signal. Am I stupid or am I not meant to notice? Or else they may not be signals at all – but just one of those things.

To put it briefly: I can get ratty and cross. I feel that these intruders have no right to use me as casually as a pair of pyjamas. At times I remember the last thought in my head before I leave. "Who the hell does he think he is?"

Probing the Soul

I do it too. Please don't think that I am just showing off. It was glorious when we were kids, and saved up a few pennies to buy some 'X-ray' glasses. We really did think that we'd be able to see girls' knickers. But we saw through their flesh as well! That was the joke. That was the image that these toys created. Now isn't it the same when you first hear about telepathy, for example? You jump at once to some pretty wild conclusions, don't you? You begin to infer a whole lot of things. This little sidestep into the realm of unreason and fear is caused by the shadows in your mind.

Can I 'read' the secret code for the petty-cash box? Can I 'recognize' which horse has decided that it's going to win the next

11

race? Am I 'aware' of who is having affairs with whom and at what address? Worse still, can I spy on the secrets of your sexuality and learn about those special extras? You didn't ask for intimacy of this sort and you're insulted that I explore your soul to such extreme depths. I am a snoop. There should be laws against it. You are angry and wild.

You do see what I mean? It is not such a boon as you might imagine. Since you can't switch it off, you learn how to repress it. You can do this by conducting one of the louder Mahler symphonies in your mind. Or else by working out how many five pound banknotes it would need to cover a rugby pitch. Then you realize what the Inland Revenue have been up to all these years. In short, if you focus your mind on a riveting problem, these psychic powers press less heavily on your brain.

It does not block them entirely though, and it makes people think you're eccentric. Your mind wanders, and you pay very little attention to what they may say. In fact, you switch your energies onto a different track to avoid offending them, and that offends them even more. "Who do you think you are," they ask, "God?"

AC went to great trouble to show me that this particular gift is crucial in one's intimate life, and in one's magical career. "It is one thing to make love at someone. It is another thing to merge your soul with theirs and glow with love like stellar incandescence."[9]

This power, also the study in Tantrism[10] and in Bakhti Yoga,[11] is paramount to occultism and magic. This is the reason that the Church is puzzled in its attitude to sex. It is the means whereby we can tap into the stream of creative energy by which everything else was composed.

"It's a pity that sex makes men either snicker or sweat," said

9. When I try to express this thought today, I refer to nuclear fusion – as contrasted with nuclear fission. His way was better, but a bit more difficult to grasp.

10. It has to be said that Tantrism arises out of Hinduism and may be regarded as the equivalent of a Black Mass to the Christian Faith. Acts which might bring about moral degradation in any normal man, enable a 'wise one' to break through to revelation. The religion claims to pre-date Hinduism itself, but it probably began only in the 10th century, A.D.

11. One of the ten recognized forms of yoga, or paths to realization. Bakhti yoga is the way of love and devotion.

Aleister. "It's simply a shame when they turn it into such a tragedy! If they would apply will, they might perceive that this way lies true communion."

Of course, most folk are very nervous on the topic. In their presence, you shut your own mind too, like closing the lid of a treasure chest. But you can't avoid sensing things. The best way is to achieve a state of emotional calm when you are detached from these things. All the same, you can see what a valuable instrument this could be. It would help to heal a marriage that is going wrong. It could aid a young person to conquer shyness, to let him master his fears.

Nightmare Figure

When so many, for so long, have called Crowley a monster, the question arises: "Is it possible he was one?"[12] The answer is no! The evidence against him is too neat. The attacks are too gross. The advocates have too much froth on their lips. They never go for his magic, you'll notice. They only ever have a go at his alleged behaviour. Besides which, I can vouch for his sincerity.

All together now – "Well you would, wouldn't you?" But that's just the point: No, I would not. Crowley was a great magician, and the fact is not changed by whatever else they might say. A better question is: why do they say it? Why go to the trouble of perpetuating the lies? We should ask the Templars and the Cathars. One destroys a man's name when one means to do him wrong.

I can settle the hash of anybody who attacks me. Aleister was a good teacher. He too, especially now that he is dead, is quite well placed for settling old scores. We sometimes join our forces together like a Family Business. It's just fun. We're only kids at heart. I try to keep a balanced view, and I do not ask for the moon or expect the Pope to declare me a Saint. Aleister was more congenial than they admit, and less sinister than they pretend. But who are 'they'? What is their motive for keeping the Crowley myth alive? Why are they furious with me for exposing his normality? They are the ones who look for power. It is why we must all be careful.

12. This phenomenon is restricted to Great Britain. Crowley's reputation carries no stigma at all on the continent or elsewhere in the world. This should lead any intelligent person to think that certain British institutions must have had a special reason for this persistent denigration.

They tried to take it from him. They tried to take it from me. The usual ploy is to hoodwink me with a very likely student. They are looking for papers. But they are also looking for a 'dance'. Yes, there is a dance. In truth it is a series of magical gestures linked together. The Hindu might call it "The Love of Lord Siva". This dance derives from forces that lie behind the Indian, the Dervish, the Spanish, and the Slav. It is the *first* dance, the one before words. It brought the world into being and it could also destroy.

Think of magic mazes cut into the turf. Think of Abra Melin's magic squares! Think of gestures of power. Think with your feet for once! How did the old song go? "I am following in my father's footsteps". And what about the carol: "In the old man's steps he trod"? Right people may do that. Right people's bodies can fill the holes in space, just like keys sliding into locks. When that dance is 'performed', it becomes a sacred ritual. The dancer is at last able to conjure and control vast energies.

They have done AC great wrong. I am calling all debts in. No man is above The Law. The Law requires that each man answer for his actions. Amado, Zadok, Hymaneus Beta ... all must give account. If you make amends, well and good. If not, then none dare stand between you and them.

The name of AC still has a deep effect. It is hated by the Masons, damned by the Vatican, and makes the blue blood of royalty froth into foam. Yet Royalty, Church and Masons must admit – the mass media pose more danger than ever Crowley did.

Lawyers do not queue up to defend AC's name. They have their careers to think of! I may be naive, but I gather crumbs of comfort from all of this. When the donkeys call you a fool, it is a very rare compliment. There is a lot to learn from reading the list of a man's enemies.

14

3

TARANIS

A Gallic God, often shown holding the wheel of chance, or a thunder-bolt

Eliphas Levi

People think that Crowley was a victim of the Tarot's magic. They are wrong. To be precise, he was more wrapped up in the man who suggested a link between the Tarot and the Cabala. His name was Eliphas Levi (1810 to 1875).[13] This man had the same impact on Aleister as Aleister has on people today. My father was so struck by this affinity, he though he might be Levi's avatar.[14]

"It had nothing to do with his body," Aleister laughed as he told me about this. "Even if I were a dragoon,[15] the man was half ordained and fully dead!" But he could not fathom the reason for his interest. "It all became clear," he laughed. "We have both been vessels for the same soul." He gave me one of his glances. "You may kiss me if you wish!"

To probe this puzzle, AC studied the Tarot very deeply. For many years he called it the 'Ptah Rota', suggesting that the cards should be read in the same way as the Egyptian 'Book of the Dead'. It was a handbook for souls who enter the next world. But he chucked this idea out. "It won't do," he said. "You cannot ask a dying man to shuffle the deck and select thirteen cards!"[16]

---

13. This was a 'nom de guerre'. He was actually the Abbé Alphonse Louis Constant and he died the same year that Crowley was born.
14. The current habitation, of some being or god who moves on from one entity to another.
15. One of the words he used for 'homosexual'. I think it was current during his own youth at Cambridge.
16. It is my own theory that the origin is 'Tarana Roteh' or 'The Wheel of the God Taranis'.

The cards could not foretell the future. But common folk had seen them being 'read', and drew the wrong conclusion. They added two and two, and made it six. But Crowley was never one to follow the mob. In the end, he disagreed with scholars who invented a tenuous link between the Tarot and the Cabala. He did not contradict them. But he did not endorse them. He felt that the Tarot hid something else. But you know how people are ... once they celebrate their secret find, they also stop looking. Left to his own devices, Crowley studied the Tarot for the whole of his life.

He did not see the Tarot as a route. He felt they might be 'keys' that opened doors at a deeper level of being. His ideas were not all that far from Sigmund Freud or Carl Gustav Jung. I would put it more simply still. The cards are like a computer which can recognize you. This is why Aleister had his own designs painted. His choice of symbols were personal to him. They tell the story of his life, and show that the work was not finished.

My grandma gave me some Tarot cards when I was thirteen. They were older than anything Crowley had seen before and they intrigued him. But I became an Initiate at fourteen, and my grandma would not let him keep the cards to study. He did admit that they upset all his theories. This is why:

- There are six suits.
- Five suits have fourteen cards.
- One suit has fifteen cards.
- The Major Arcana has twenty-eight cards.
- Each of the one hundred and thirteen cards has a unique design.

The average estimate of their age is three hundred years. On the whole, they are in good state. A few have a corner missing, and one was torn by a child. When my own mother was a little girl, she pasted yellow stars on the reverse sides. I had an even worse idea. I varnished them.

It would be nice if I could reproduce these cards. I'd be very willing. I have no reason to keep them private. I have a partial set of colour slides that I use to give lectures. The real problem is cost. My editor did some quick sums on a pocket calculator. He was so quick, I thought he was masturbating. But the result was: "Forget it!" So I cannot put my grandma's Tarot within reach. I prefer to keep prices down and hold on to my readers. Unlike some American books, I do not try to rob you. I want to reach people. I have some magical goals to achieve.

In 1972, I was offered £5,000 for these cards. Today, twenty years later, they must be worth at least ten times more. The offer came from a pop star. He had so much money, he had become allergic to the stuff. He said he was very keen on the occult. He was one of AC's best fans. Which made me wonder why he kept his soul in his wallet. He needed my cards for personal reasons but he was damned if he was going to bid more. Fame is often an evil prize. One starts to cherish gold and throw away the elixir of life. I told him that things can only be exchanged if their value was the same. He should have given me something else.

I told him what to do with his money. To judge by his last photo, he did it too.

Gazing at Stars

I can't blame people for reaching the Tarot by the wrong route. I can't reproach them if they go down the wrong path. Too much has been said and written. In these days of futility, and these nights of despair, I shall not take food from Tarot readers' mouths. They must eat. "Spectacle frames and lenses can be very costly," Aleister said. "Vision is given free."[17] To see the Tarot, you may have to un-learn things. So many books have been written in the last hundred years. Before that though, not a dicky-bird. Strange, eh? Yes, the Tarot existed, but only as a game. Only as late as the late 1800s did it become a playful way of reading the future. Even then, it was taken as lightly as the little curls of paper one gets in Christmas crackers!

There are pictures and drawings from the 13th century. They show Kings of France and other notables playing at this game of cards. There is no occult meaning. We have other drawings which show how simple it was to use a mediaeval toilet. You sat with your backside over the ramparts and aimed mainly at the moat.

---

17. Does it help at all to know that clinical psychologists use a series of imaginative cards to help diagnose certain mental conditions? It is called 'The Thematic Apperception Test', or TAT.

Tough luck for the dawn fishers. Since our ancestors had no other use for these cards, who suggested there was one?

In Paris, in 1397, the cards were banned as being a distraction from work. There was no breath or hint of anything hermetic until 1770, when Antoine, Comte de Gébelins, mused that they looked a bit like Egyptian signs. A certain 'Eteilla'[18] saw the potential; he pushed the idea of Egypt as far as he could and the thing became a craze. In the mid 1850s, our old friend, Eliphas Levi, got bitten by the bug. By his time though, the signs of Egypt had been decoded and – alas, alas – there was no connection with the Tarot!

It was Eliphas Levi who hustled the Cabala on to the occult scene of Europe. Before that, it was just a form of theoretic mysticism used by the Jews and not much by anyone else. But the Jews strove to edge Judaism in to Magic, and did anything they could to attract the eye. In spite of all this, in mediaeval times magic was mostly to do with Alchemy, the art of numbers and sorcery. If you missed the reference in my first book, AC had no great liking for the Jews.

"Why are the seven stars no more than seven?" asks the Jester of King Lear. "Because they are not eight!" answers the mad King. The Jester taunts: "Thou wouldst have made a good fool, nuncle!" Did Shakespeare know that they had got the planets wrong? The truth of Chaldea was about to be proven false. "Uranus?" screamed the Alchemists in 1781. "Neptune?" howled the Astrologers in 1846. In the year of my birth, 1930, "Pluto?" shrieked the shades of the Golden Dawn. Now we have Charon too. But does it faze them? Not at all. Two weeks – and they have calculated the truth anew.

This happened when Eliphas Levi came up with a new idea. In his case though, there was no evidence. He just printed a strange theory which coupled the cards of the Tarot with the letters of the Hebrew alphabet, and thence the Cabala. Now Levi did not speak a word of Hebrew, apart from "Amen"! But he didn't let that stand in his way.

Levi's new proposals brought a breath of fresh air into the stale world of occultism. His ideas were drawn together by Dr Gerard Encausse, also known as 'Papus'.[19] The impact was similar to that

18. i.e., Alliete.
19. He lived 1865 to 1916; see 'The Tarot of the Bohemians', 1889.

18

of a washing machine today. No one asked if it was valid. It was too bloody useful. So, from that day to this, no one has ever doubted this imaginary link. It has been swallowed whole by the 'Western Occult Tradition' ... which they all claim has existed since time began.

Son of a King's Surveyor
In my opinion, a lot of the work had already been done by the man he regarded as his Teacher. This was an elderly member of the Polish nobility, Joseph Marie Hoëné Wronski, (1776 to 1853). This gentleman was the son of the official engineer to the last King of Poland, and became a French subject in 1800.[20] A scholar of great talent, he went to Greenwich to win a prize offered by the Board of Longitude. He had penned a new and reliable formula by which ships might reckon their position at sea. Sad to say, his work was printed in 'The Nautical Almanac' but he was never paid for it. He went back to Paris to work as a school teacher.

The greatest step made by Wronski was to produce the idea of 'The Absolute', i.e., the knowledge of truth attained by pure reason alone. He also drew and made up a 'machine' which could figure the harmonies that existed between two sets of numbers. He showed Levi that there did exist a primary type of liaison between the Tarot Cards and the Zodiac. We ought not to be too excited by this. Even as a simple game, cards must have a numeric basis. What is not commonly realized is that Wronski was the original author of 'The Book of the Sacred Magic of Abra-Melin the Mage'.[21]

But after Wronski's death, Levi went one step further, added the bit about the Cabala, and virtually threw away the discovery made by Wronski. We must recall that Levi was a 'silenced' priest[22] (1836) but he rejoined Solesmes (1839) to beg a penance.

20. Philippe d'Arcy, 'Wronski – Pages choisies', Seghers, 1970.
21. The title of the French Manuscript in the Bibilothèque de l'Arsenal (MS.2351) is actually: 'La sacrée magic que Dieu donna à Moyse Aaron David Salomon, et à d'autres patriarches et prophètes, qui enseigne la vraye sapience divine, laissé par Abraham à Lamech son fils, traduite en hebreu 1458.' As Ellic Howe remarked, in 'The Magicians of the Golden Dawn', 1972: "It is most unlikely that the MS has a Jewish provenance. The French text may well have been written towards the end of the seventeenth century." No, it was the end of the 18th century.
22. The Catholic equivalent of a defrocked clergyman.

19

Oddly enough, his own interest in magic had been first awakened by the private concerns of the Abbot of his old seminary. All his life, Levi was devoured by a deep interest in the use of symbols and images. He was just the right man to support Wronski – but quite unsuited to coax the Tarot into flower.

In the late 18th Century, in Poland, there was a surge of Jewish renewal. It was called 'Hasidism',[23] and was led by one Israel Baal Shem[24] (1700 – 1760). A main ploy was to turn the Cabala into a very popular pastime. As thousands of Jews emigrated to France, they took this new feature of the Cabala with them. There it passed through the romantic mind of Eliphas Levi, only to become the focus of a later craze in ritual magic.

One can judge how keenly new ideas are adopted by looking at the work of a eminent writer. Christine Hartley[25] had an item on 'The Tarot' in the weekly magazine called 'Man, Myth and Magic'.[26] In her first paragraph she says:

"It may be described as 'the cosmic method in universal creation or emanation, including its purpose and result'. As practised by the Western user, it is generally associated with the Tree of Life of the Cabala, but it has also affinities with the pyramids of Egypt and with Indian theosophical philosophy."

When I first read these words, I felt she was talking about a vintage wine. I found the language far too lofty for a magazine which was on sale to the general public. Surely, the idea was to make wisdom open. But she was murkier still when it came to matters of fact.

"The origins of the Tarot are not clearly defined. A. E. Waite concluded that it had no exoteric history before the 14th century and the oldest examples of Tarot cards probably date from about 1390, while occult tradition places their origin at about 1200 A.D. It is said that the Gypsies are believed to hold the first set of cards and that they alone hold the secret of its meaning ... According to occultists, the system comes first from the East, probably Chaldea..."

23. The word 'Hasid' means: one who is steadfast. cf. Lou Newman, 'A Hasidic Anthology', Bailey Bros, 1963.
24. Originally Israel ben Eliezer. The new name means 'Master of the Good Name'.
25. A great fan of Dion Fortune and author of 'The Western Mystery Tradition'.
26. BPC Publications Ltd, 1972-73.

Note the start of one sentence: "It is said that the Gypsies are believed to hold ..." Cast an eye on the very next one too: "According to the occultists..." The lady may be very informed, but she is not ready to commit herself. She does not say "this is", "that's why," or "therefore". Look again at the first of the two quotes: "it may be described," "it is generally associated", "it has affinities."

The article closes by telling us that no writer says quite the same thing. Hence we should read widely, and learn to imagine more. I'm afraid she forgets one simple fact. The major arcana of most tarot packs may contain twenty-two cards. Yet this isn't true over the whole of Europe. My own pack consists of one hundred and thirteen cards and is not unique. It resembles the ones that were hand-made for the Duke of Milan in 1415,[27] among several others. But you notice that she has swallowed Eliphas Levi's bait – hook, line, and sinker. In the space of one hundred years, one man's idle fancies have been hallowed into the shining truth.

What I'm really telling you is that printers edited the Major Arcana and discarded all pictures on the lesser arcana. Why on earth should they do that? Simply to get round the problem I described at the start of this chapter – to cut down on costs!

You probably don't realize that the mystic centre of your domicile – your personal Tarot cards – is as 'hermetic' as a dog's dinner. There is scarcely any point in my talking about all the 'new' packs of cards with such sublime fresh designs. They have dropped straight into the very same trap, and thus prove that "too little" knowledge is a dangerous thing. Do they give you vision or make you a seer? Are they a mystic portal to the other world? No, I'm afraid not. Well, not any more than your common set of birthday cards. But quite often, they are very pretty.

27. Jan Woudhuysen, 'Tarotmania', Wildwood House 1979.

4

ZALTYS

The grass-snake, revered by the ancient
Lithuanians as the envoy of the gods

Freak Shows

Travelling fairs used not to be like those of today. They had side
shows with monsters, freaks, and the strongest man in the world.
A woman with two heads shouted "Come on" to a bashful sailor.
"I'll give you a kiss in stereo!" But she didn't say kiss and he went
red as a beetroot. Maybe such things were fakes. I used to hope
they were. One had doubts but one couldn't be sure. But wasn't
that the whole point – the wonder and uncertainty? We didn't
care. We wanted a boost and we found it on risky rides and in
dimly lit booths. Chips were twice the normal price.

We all went on the Ghost Train though we swore we were not
scared. We secretly hoped for something awful – that a tableau
would come to life, or we would glimpse something lewd. We
tried to be older and dropped our voices to buy tickets for the
'Exotic Indian Dancing Girls'. They knew. Those posters about
anyone under sixteen being banned, huh! The girl who sold
tickets narrowed her eyes. When we'd gone in, she grinned. We
had a good night out. The people made a living.

It was just the same when crop circles first began to appear. We
did not know that this would be their label. We just called them
"something funny at Bert's place". The local papers were the first
to make a story. Before you could spit, aerial photos were taken,
and the village got a mention on TV.

We once had a cat trapped in a drain pipe. A thousand
mediums came to bring peace to the poltergeist! It was a bit like
that with these crop rings. The main debate was about the odd

patterns. But suddenly, scores of people had seen something in the sky. One man got himself beamed on board. "We had a grand chat," he said mysteriously. As luck would have it, they spoke good English, albeit with a slight Wiltshire accent.

There is one thing that you can say about Wiltshire. There seems to be a lot of it. Much of it was so empty, the Army decided to use it for a training ground. But there is Stonehenge, Avebury, and lots and lots of tumuli. It is not exactly packed with industry. Tourism would be a very good thing to develop. So if an alien vessel were looking for somewhere to park, this county is quite close to Glastonbury[28] – and all that that entails. The spacemen, or the country folk, had a quite uncanny sense of where things would do most good. Not an army parade ground, not an air force landing strip ... but "Bert's place".

Kiosks sprouted in the night, and you could soon buy postcards, models of the UFO, and those same costly chips. Nobody was a bit surprised when other rings began to flower in other fields. Some people quickly became 'experts' and stated that signs of the zodiac were in these imprints. Which is itself very strange, since the signs of the zodiac differ in every continent. Then to cap it all, someone became an official Prophet from Venus. He had been living amongst us for years in disguise. He gave notice of a galactic meeting the coming Saturday night.

"Why Saturday?" asked a pit-bull terrier from the TV News.

"They know our customs," came the grave reply. "They come when most people are free."

"Is it before the news, or after the football match?" the reporter insisted.

"In between," said the man, proving that sarcasm was lost on him.

It is this same lack of guile that is often a feature of schizophrenia. One hesitates to give them tablets since they are so obviously enjoying a state of mindless bliss. They too are quite able to communicate with 'higher beings' without the use of a telephone or a CB. I do not suggest that UFO watchers are mad. My theory is that perhaps mental illness is being wrongly diagnosed. It is just possible that the ones we turn into patients are actually 'under guidance'. They even tell us so themselves.

28. A small town that is crammed with myths and legends, and which has become almost the 'hippy' Jerusalem.

Events in step

Of course, the facts of science are not in his favour. I will give an example. The nearest other star is approximately 4·3 *light* years away. This means that our visitors had to plan things a long time in advance. In fact, when they set off, Wiltshire did not exist, and human beings had not yet invented Saturday. Besides which, having gone to all that trouble and expense – the best method they can find to communicate with us, is to leave incomprehensible signs imprinted in our bleeding food crops!

"Ah," say the converted, "they have the technology"! But no, they don't. Or if they do, it bears a very close resemblance to that seen in 'Star Wars', 'Star Trek' and 'Terminator 2'. That is to say: they never possess a thing that has not previously been imagined by man. Look back in recent history. Start with Jules Verne or H. G. Wells. Ever since, men have been seeing or meeting beings from 'outer space' – the verbal traffic is modern, the clothing is of the period, and the vehicle itself is exactly what we would expect.

Before we knew about black holes, neither did they. Before we made nuclear power, they ran their vessels on anti-gravity stuff. Before Planck and Einstein, they travelled 'faster than the speed of light'. Perhaps they have come just to steal our ideas before we patent them.

Odd how 'they' can cure all illness, speak in every tongue, and perform every type of miracle. One might say that they embody all the hopes and dreams that mankind has ever had. If one accepts them at face value, they are 'proof' that existence is more than we feared. They bring us hope. They bring us reason to hope. If we need that hope, we are not about to ask too many penetrating questions. We will believe first. Afterwards, there will be no doubt. And who knows? There might be a fat lady with two heads!

The same 'agents' who prop up the UFO craze have been behind many other cults in the past. For example, there was once a mass movement to show public penitence for one's sins.[29] It began in Perugia, in Italy, during the late 13th century. Within very few years, it had spread through the rest of Europe. People had found a futile method of dealing with The Great Plague.

29. The Brotherhood of Flagellants.

Thousands joined the cult in the vain hope of cheating the angel of death.

They used to give advance notice of towns and dates. They would then gather in their thousands, strip to the waist, and flog each other for exactly thirty-three and a half days. They used whips of knotted thongs in which metal shards had been inserted. You don't need to know much about S & M[30] to realize what the "great rush of purifying ecstasy" was. Even after they'd been cleansed, they kept at it till another rush came. It sounds a bit like modern Marxism, hmm?

Gerald Gardner tried to install this kind of lashing in modern 'wicca'.[31] He said it was quite normal when someone new became a pagan. The covens who have adopted the practice are more popular than the ones who keep it simple. Since it is all done 'sky-clad', or naked, men learn to avoid areas of high pressure to the south.

People who are mentally ill are often glad to talk about their symptoms, but are less eager to hear your thoughts about it. They want to pull you into their reality. They have no wish to join you in yours. When you study their case notes, it is shocking to find how slight was 'the last straw' that broke them. They fell ill for no reason at all. One wonders, did they wish to be deranged? Did they seek it? Did they open up and invite the nightmare to gallop in? Like suicide, it almost seems that they did it to themselves.

A typical feature of schizophrenia is that the sick man thinks you are ill, and not him. Did you happen to see me in the late sixties? I was with ten others, chasing a naked young man along the Reading Road.

"Why did you run?" asked the police. "Because they were chasing me," he said. "Why had you taken your clothes off?" "I hadn't put them on." "Do you like to be nude?" "I'm always nude, under my clothes."

Do you get it? We were the ones asking stupid questions. He had bluffed his way out of hospital three times already. The first time, he was seen eating a cat. The second time, he climbed a roof to pee on electric cables. The third time, he tried to paint the Town Hall red. As I said, he cannot see why your reality is any better than his. He can feel his. Therefore it is genuine.

30. Sadomasochism.
31. It is the title which witches themselves prefer to the flat term witchcraft.

25

Probable Causes

A bizarre thing about crop circles: they don't occur in China. Nor in Russia. They don't happen anywhere except where people have read about them. There's ample space in Tibet, or the Gobi Desert. There's room in the Australian outback, or the pampas of Argentina. But there are no buses. Fewer family cars. Not much point landing a UFO where you can't drum up an audience. Because that's the other point: the chaps from space have a taste for publicity.

No offence. But like the Virgin Mary, UFOs tend to manifest where they are likely to be welcome. They have offered all kinds of mystic explanation, but why avoid the obvious one? This brings back a childhood memory. "I know something you don't know!" I was a spoil-sport even then. "Why don't you grow up?" I used to ask.

Sadly, no one puts his beliefs to the acid test by trying to convince a healthy, genuine sceptic. They do tests, of course – their own tests, their own way, with results that suit their purpose. Like the widow to whom any creak is her husband's ghost, Ufology has all the zeal it takes to misinterpret the facts. But if these things were truly UFOs, they would read more like science and less like science fiction.

If there were life elsewhere in our universe, most likely it would be inferior. It takes time to develop. This is why the age of the cosmos is relevant.[32] All creation is expanding outward and our own distance from the centre has the right conditions. Any superior race would be further away, and far too cold. Any inferior race would be nearer the centre, and would still look like a mushroom. Of course, there could just be a parallel planet, the same distance from the centre but on the opposite side of the perimeter. The time it would take to get here, the cosmos would have collapsed.

Either one claims a sort of divinity for these creatures, or one gives them credit for waiting until the American elections were over!

It is a spiffing lure – if they spoke to you and nobody else! Just fancy. They went over the heads of all statesmen and qualified scientists just to talk to you about destiny. And maybe

32. cf. J.Gribbin & M.Rees, 'The Stuff of the Universe', Heinemann, 1977.

26

it somehow 'altered' you – their touch, I mean. Is this the truth at last? Do Ufologists mutate in order to be ready for their future galactic role? With such a splendiferous future in the bag, why do they push their magazines? Why do they need new members?

It is always a give away when a theory is proof against any and every objection. It replaces 'reason' with 'conviction'. Above all, it gets so furious with anyone who voices doubts. In their eyes, I am a doubting fool. So why get angry with me? I thought Gods would be like 'Vulcans' and rise above emotions. Now if I am to be reasonable, then I have to confess – it's difficult proving that someone didn't spend Christmas on Venus, if he said he did.[33] But you may know about logic. It is very rarely possible to prove a negative. Then it's tricky showing he didn't. Nobody can prove a negative!

Crop rings were so vital to people, that when even after hoaxers confessed, they just ignored them as fools. In theological terms, their claims are absurd. From an occult point of view, the claims are foolish and unnecessary. Why seek to explain that which is already accepted as truth? They should copy the O.T.O. or the Golden Dawn and just stay aloof. Be blind, be deaf, and whisper in folk's ear-holes. Best of all: spread rumours. That is the best occult strategy of all.

How long will the average pilgrim wait at the gates of Jerusalem? How long can a soul survive without a whiff of hope? It is not going to happen. You know it. I know it. But I wonder how you dare sell it, when you know you will have to explain? As AC said: "Only special kinds of people try to cheat the Gods!"

That is why I always sniff the air for sulphur, so to speak. You are misled and dangerous. Other things being equal, I will see you fall and leave the scene. Please. No frothing at the mouth! I am quite aware of the trap I have dug. "Ha-ha!" you shout. "But the devil you imply is even less likely to exist than the UFOs." Is it so?

---

33. Velikovsky made just such a claim, I believe. But he never explained how their biology could function in the greater heat of the planet Venus, nor why, if they could travel, they didn't migrate to earth. The answer is, of course, one cannot order them to provide proof. Naturally.

– He has been around much longer.
– Very few people wish to deny him.
– He could turn fields into corn flakes.
– In sceptical times, he would use madness.
– Mental illness is rocketing.

Toy-Shop Magic

It's easy to set up shop as a psychic. I'm amazed that more don't do it. It is extremely common in France. Even up-market magazines carry pages of publicity. A cosy chat on the telephone will set you back about twenty pounds. Or they will interpret an imprint of your buttocks for a fee of fifty pounds. They used to sell oodles of magic jewellery until one lady went to prison. To judge by the claims of certain perfumes, she may just have changed her product line.

In England, it is illegal to pretend to read the future. But it takes very few weeks to win a diploma in heart massage, eye-ball gazing, or Aura Astral Art. All you need is a public eager to believe in something. They will pay anything for a nice sensation. That's mostly how it is with youth. How does it feel?

In contrast to UFOs, tarot cards, and Welsh harps, etc, have you noticed how 'serious magic' is located higher up the social ladder? I'm not an elitist. Some of my critics say that I should be. How dare I bring down the tone! Who do I think I am to break the valuable mystique! I am excluded from the Royal Enclosure at Ascot ... but I have also been declared 'persona non grata' in a travellers' squat. I shouldn't brag. My act goes down like a lead zeppelin!

5

VODNIK

A demon of the water who lures Slavs to their death. He is lulled by the gift of a chicken[34]

Witness

After my first book, in May 1991, I got many letters. Some of them were abusive, a few were affable, and one or two came from a mental hospital. One man, who gave his name as 'God', accused the staff of keeping him hostage. He wanted me to send a tubular steel ladder of the type used by 'James Bond'. "It is soon my birthday," he pointed out. I answer letters when I can, but not those who fail to enclose return postage. I did not send 'God' His tubular ladder. I looked, Oh Lord, but found not.

I was pleased when an old gentleman wrote to me from the West Country. He had been present at the great ritual when we enticed Rudolf Hess to England. He had been in the Intelligence Corps and he guarded one of the highest radio towers of the day. He was also supposed to make 'illicit' radio calls to a mate. The scripts for this were delivered every day. It amused him to think of the poor boffins[35] who hoped to win the war by composing the stuff.

Voice A　What are the women like, down your way, Bert?

Voice B　There are some real smashers, I can tell you. Trouble is, they're all picked up by the bleeding Yanks. You know how much money their boys get paid.

---

34. Hence the popularity (among European Jews and others) of 'chicken soup to warm the soul'. In Russian his name is 'vodyanoi'.
35. A technical expert. This slang word was said to come from "back off inside."

Voice A   What the hell are the Yanks doing down your way? They were supposed to have come up here, closer to London.

Voice B   Well they landed at Sotton[36] OK but without any road signs, the sods took a left and went down into Devon. They're having to shuttle fuel down to get them back.

Voice A   I bet the driver in the first tank got it in the neck, eh?

Voice B   You what? He got a perishing medal. (Etc.)

The aim of this sprightly dialogue was to mislead the enemy. It was known they detected all radio activity in the south of England. The 'duff gen' had to be scattered through the scripts with very great care so as not to rouse German suspicions.

In the week leading up to the ritual, they were ordered to keep a special look-out. By climbing up the tower, of course, he also got a good view of the goings-on in and around the church. The man tells me that not twenty miles away was a large group of Canadian troops. At great expense, the Canadian government had sent out a theatre troupe, with some of the most popular stars of the day. To fill the long days of total silence, the Canadian ladies had been ordered to cut and sew some occult costumes! The material they used was salvaged from faulty parachutes. Yards of it were also smuggled out. All along the south coast, soldiers walked out with girls in new, bouffant dresses.

One other morsel of news: on the night of the ritual, my informant grew a little too curious and sneaked a glance through the bushes. He saw a large cluster of people doing "pretty weird things", while "this airplane mock-up zoomed over, covered in flame". Then someone with his face painted ordered him to "piss off", and he went back to his radio routines.

This adds little to my own account,[37] but it confirm that the events occurred. Army personnel put on weird robes and there was a mock airplane. This verifies two points in my story. Now, shall Military Intelligence continue to deny the rest? If so, what do they suggest that the army was up to? Not a Gay Rights party?

36. An argot name for Southampton.
37. 'The Secrets of Aleister Crowley', Diamond Books, 1991.

A Templar Link

Later on, as a driver at the War Ministry, this same man brought important people down from London to Hastings, to visit AC. Most of them were top brass, including a General, but he heard them refer to one as Mr Gerald Yorke. I do not know if Gerald Yorke did any military service, but my friend insists that all the persons wore staff uniforms. When they reached the place where Crowley lived, the old man was very ill and received them in his bedroom. After some thirty minutes of close discussion, the visitors went into some other room, to give AC some peace. The simple soldier was left alone with the frail magician and felt rather nervous.

He needn't have worried at all. Crowley smiled at him kindly and his eyes seemed to pierce the soldier's soul. The young man went closer, sat on the bed, and they started to chat like old friends. When he had finished, Crowley opened his wallet and handed him a piece of paper. "I'm sorry to say that I've nothing finer to offer." As a matter of fact, it was a scrappy, old pawn ticket. "Throw it away, if you want," said Aleister. "Or go down town and redeem it. It will cost you a shilling or two!" The young man excused himself and left the room.

A nursing sister had just served the officers with tea, so he guessed he had enough time. He hurried down to Hastings in the official car, and coughed up ten pounds to redeem the object that Crowley had pawned. The owner of the shop produced the famous 'Baphomet ring' which was made of pure gold and an intaglio setting. On returning to the house, he tried to press it on to the old man. "No, no," said Crowley "I have no need. It served its purpose so I ask for no more."

Acting on a kindly impulse, the young soldier gave Crowley the last twenty pounds in his pocket. The old man was quite reluctant to take it. But when the other fellow insisted, Aleister smiled and hid it under the sheets. "It will come in handy," he murmured. "There are so many glorious things they don't want me to have!" There was a wicked old twinkle in his eye.

Now that word, Baphomet, is ever so odd. Of course, anybody worth his salt believes it is the name of a 'heretical idol' that the Knights Templar were said to have revered. At least, that was one of the principal reasons given by the Pope for their massacre. It 'proved' that they were heretics, and by also accusing them of sodomy, it proved they were the foulest kind of heretics. For good measure, he said they ate babies too!

But this is not just a childish play on that fearful word 'Mahomet'. This is derived from a Hebrew word, *'behema'*, meaning 'an animal', and *'behemoth'* meaning a monster. A German author, one of the great experts on such matters, has pointed out[38] that *'Baphomet'* is a symbol for 'the ineffable name of God'.

This is tough luck on all those people who accuse AC of being a Satanist. It's hard cheese for those who 'imitate' him by forming groups that love to practice black magic. If anything, my friends, the Baphomet Ring supports the notion that AC was very advanced on the road of Gnostic truth.

King of Witches

The same man also knew 'Dr' Gerald Gardner very well. You must remember him from my first book. He was the chap with sexual problems who helped to construct the dear cult of the witches. I am happy to say that he endorses everything I said. He went further. He gave me other insights into that man's true nature.

Yes, it is true that Gardner was obsessed by sex. He bought a plot of land in Hampstead, that was next to a nudist club. He had an old cottage pulled down, piece by piece, and rebuilt close to the boundary wall. Beside spying on the nudists, he used this tiny cottage as a temple. The altar was a zinc table from a kitchen. Behind it, the 'holy of holies' was veiled from view by a blanket. All quite apt, since the inner sanctum was simply an old spring mattress laid on the floor!

As for Gardner's 'Museum of Witchcraft', he got that by fraud. It belonged to a man I shall call Mr Claude Forster.[39] Gardner came by one weekend and stayed for several months. During this time, he claimed that he had received a telegram from a 'Lady Fiddler'. She was keen to present her own 'superb collection' to the museum. In due course a crate arrived, containing kitchen pots and pans. A touch of interest had been added in the shape of runic symbols, hammered in with the head of a nail.

---

38. Manfred Lurker. 'Lexikon der Götter und Dämonen', 1984, Alfred Krämer Verlag, Stuttgart.
39. Once again, I protect my sources by giving a 'cover' name.

Then 'Lady Fiddler' arrived at Douglas airport. Once again, the news came by telegram which only Gardner saw. Spending money for the first time since taking up residence, he went alone to meet their eminent guest. Claude Forster got a clear whiff of a rat.

The great lady duly arrived and, being weary from pedalling the airplane, went upstairs to her room. Now there was a small restaurant joined to the museum. As visitors left the display, they found themselves wandering between plates of cakes and tea-cups. A shy waitress, a local girl, beckoned urgently to Claude Forster. She was upset and couldn't quite find the words for what she had to say. "That Lady," she blurted. "She isn't no lady. Me and her worked in Douglas. We was both tarts."

At breakfast, next morning, they had toast and a furious row. Gardner had a devious plan to get rid of Forster and take the Museum over. Since this was Forster's only means of income, he offered to sell it, cash down, or Gardner and his 'lady' would wend their way to the Hebrides. They paid two thousand pounds, which was far less than the business was worth.

This same Mr Forster confirms that the witch rituals, the 'Book of Shadows' and the rest were indeed written by AC, just as I said. The dear, old Dr Gardner just 'titivated the English' in an effort to make it sound ancient. In fact, he was a bloody fool for ever tackling this. There are words current today which did not exist a couple of centuries ago. There are words which were used in quite a another way. What is more, the style of speech and writing was distinct and words were in a different order. To get away with that kind of forgery, you really must be one of the experts.

No matter how Gardner got the title of doctor, he was no ex-pert on the English language. It was the faults that he introduced which finally gave the show away. As I explained earlier,[40] it was thi. that helped the research[41] at the University of Santa Barbara to expose the fraud.

When I first wrote about all this, quite a few people thought I was talking through my hat. It is a great comfort to have this direct proof. Mr Forster was a witness to most of these events and makes a valued addition to the story.

40. In my first book: 'The Secrets of Aleister Crowley'.
41. cf. Professor Jeffrey B. Russell, 'A History of Witchcraft', 1980, Thames & Hudson.

Sorcery Today

Witches may be sad to hear this news, though they should have suspected it for a long time. It must seem that I dwell on the subject, or that I mount 'my attacks' with glee. No. I mock those authors who try to scorn AC when they are quite aware of the truth. But I've had my say. I shan't rub salt in the wounds. How nice if they had apologized. But that would have been asking for the moon! Don't blame me for their dilemma. I did not cause it – I only exposed it. Oops, sorry!

AC did what he did at the behest of Gerald Gardner, who paid him! You should use your heads and stop trying to cover up the mistake. Crowley needed the extra cash, but what was Gardner after? How wrong of you to despise one and pardon the other. How stupid to walk up 'Gardner's Path' when I have shown where it leads. But that's your own affair. I retaliate against those who lash out at AC. Let's ignore the press. God knows, you've had your fair share of bad publicity too! When all is said and done, he was a Master. That is why he gave you a mystic door-way.

Oh, I feel sympathy. I see how crushing it is when you are told your religion is a sham charade. You were secure in your beliefs. You liked the rituals. You found help and solace for ills of the soul. And so you feel that I have kicked you in the teeth! I do understand. But please don't try to patch over the holes with more 'fresh' evidence. It would still be a lie and your worship would still be in vain. Truth is a great sifter of souls. There is no real comfort in lies, nor any fount of peace in a Garden of Pretence.

For instance, it is quite improper to go from witch to pagan priestess and thence to Earth Mother. Yes, these things may well have existed, but there simply are not the linkages that you require. Be truthful in your own souls, at least. A thing does not become true just because it would be very helpful! If you would like it otherwise, there is nothing at all you can do. It does your cause no good to grin at your quandary. It does worse than no good to suppose that the Goddess, as you conceive her, will intercede at all in your affairs.

You know this, in your hearts. That other world is way beyond a mauling by Women's Lib! Find a way that is worthy of your deepest desires and do not lie your way to equality. You have no need. You are not, never were, separate beings – but you have lost track of your timeless link with Man. You yearn for the magical union of two spirits, but I counsel you to ransack the universe for a spirit that was divided into two.

Be brave, sisters. Have faith, brothers. God may be a Goddess and there may be more than one. But we are all children of Truth. You suspect me, I do not blame you for that. But I have no wish to replace your leaders or to poach your people. I want to uproot the tares. I want to tear out the weeds. I wish to see AC's work bear fruit. I am not your enemy. Were you to show a modicum of respect, I could quench your thirst and load your caravan with wisdom. The desert would be much smaller as you rode home. You could walk with me on my path, or you could take some other track, just as you chose.[42]

There is no doctrine in the witch faith. It was not to Gardner's taste and it wasn't on his shopping list. But there is the key to a doctrine. The problem is that so many amateurs have tried to adjust things. This is why witches do, but do not succeed. Did you never spot it? They don't teach either. There's nothing to teach. As for hidden mysteries, they don't exist! One goes for a good time and thrills. I do not doubt that one can be inspired and deeply convinced. So can door to door salesmen.

---

42. Do not write c/o of the publishers. Use the following address without adding my name: BM-Box 77, London WC1N 3XX. Although I travel about Europe, my friends will forward any non-offensive letters at top speed. Return postage in the form of a self-addressed envelope with an International Reply Paid Coupon would be a courtesy.

6
TIR

The Armenian god of writing, wisdom and oracles

Dennis Wheatley

As Shakespeare said:[43] "some men are born great, some achieve greatness, and some have greatness thrust upon them." In the case of the late Dennis Wheatley, there ought to be a fourth category: those who willingly sell their soul for greatness – then vainly try to snatch it back! As I said before, I did once write to Wheatley. It was when I was doing my National Service and I was in the R.A.F.

He knew of me, he said, and for no obvious reason announced that he'd enjoyed the rank of Wing Commander. Even in those days I had my naughty sense of humour, so I wrote back and thanked him for having had the courage to confess. This seemed to turn on his ignition. He did not lay very great store on the fact that I was Crowley's son. He was just very cross that I was not properly impressed and that I did not grovel. He went on to tell me that he had done nothing whatever to feel guilty about!

This emotional outburst gave me pause to think. Certainly it had the very opposite effect to the one he hoped to create. He never wrote to me again. In view of how close to the truth I had come, albeit by accident, I can't say that I blamed him. I must have provoked some pain – or maybe even some sieving of his soul. All the same, he did rather ask for it. We must not forget that he made quite a pretty penny out of his 'occult fiction' and much more still from the films that followed. In all of this work, he sought, and was given, an enormous amount of help by AC.

---

43. Twelfth Night, II, iv.

Yet he too ended his days by stepping back from, and even denying, his former friend.

In a later book, entitled 'The Devil and All His Works',[44] there are various plates. Beneath a snapshot of my father, he writes: 'Aleister Crowley, who claimed to be the Devil's chief emissary on earth.'! How strange that he should go so far out of his way to be so scathing. In any case, he is quite wrong. Much depends on what this or that person means by 'the devil', doesn't it? Even more depends on what one wishes to convey by the words 'chief emissary'.

But what Wheatley was actually doing, of course, was skirting to the edge before somebody took a school photo. He was inching away, trying to give another picture, trying to prove that he'd had far less to do with the same Crowley whom he was about to betray. Wheatley had rejoined the church and was doing a fair imitation of Saint Peter and his famous cock. You know the one I mean. It crowed thrice.

No, I am not being unfair. In the same book, there is a photograph of Crowley's own 'Magick in Theory and Practice'. Out of pure vanity, Wheatley has left it open at the title page. There we can read AC's words in his own hand: 'To Dennis Wheatley in memory of the sublime Hungarian banquet.' The said Dennis had regaled Crowley to dinner at a restaurant called 'The Gay Hussar'. But to make things perfectly clear, the same hand has altered the wording on the title page. The words 'published by' have been crossed out and replaced by the new words 'Published for Dennis Wheatley'.

Viewed in the kindest possible light, all this does rather suggest a relationship that was somewhat close. At the very least, the two of them were more intimate than, say, 'strangers in the night'. In spite of his new dislike of 'the devil's emissary', dear Dennis had not chucked this first edition into his old dustbin. It had gained a certain value in terms of hard cash.

Wheatley was in the Secret Services during the war, along with Ian Fleming and several others who also became authors. As a matter of fact, it was this same Dennis Wheatley who first brought Crowley to the notice of the one and only Winston Churchill.[45] What a mad, mad world, my masters!

44. Wheatley, Dennis. 'The Devil and All His Works', Hutchinson & Co. 1971.
45. Howard, Michael. 'The Occult Conspiracy' Rider & Co. 1989

Phantasm

Well, it is not my place to judge a man's scruples – although I do believe that they will be judged, one day. I do not go along with the pious Christian idea: that all sins are forgiven by true remorse – even when that remorse comes at the last minute. What is the point of such a doctrine? What does such a get-out clause do for mankind? It offers hope precisely to those who do not deserve it. "Though your sins be as scarlet, they shall be as white as snow!" Or so says the prophet Isaiah. That's as may be, but I suspect there is a big 'IF' hidden somewhere.

And how does that apply to Judas Iscariot or to any other man who first makes his thirty (thousand) pieces of silver and then betrays his friend? Does it still exist, by the way – The Potter's Field?

This is what AC said:

"It does not look at all genteel to see anxious but repentant men, pounding their breasts and shrieking 'Not mine, O Lord, but his the blame!"

Or then again: "One fine day they'll notice," he said, all but singing the famous aria from Madame Butterfly. "They'll notice the heavy footfall of the court usher. It is the goddess Maat, the lady of truth, whose walk is normally as light as a feather. When they raise their fearful eyes, they'll see her nod. They shall have no choice then. Then shall they rue their sins. For they must pass before the seat of Judgement and hear what Osiris says. And in the eyes of Osiris shall be mirrored their own."

No, I don't think he meant to be taken literally. To judge by his manner, he was mixing his metaphors and much enjoying it.

When I speak of the things that secret agents want to take away from me, everyone assumes that I am talking about certain papers. But there is much more to it than that. For example, among other things, I possess the following:

- Membership lists of the Masons around the year 1900;
- A list of CIA agents sneaked in to the O.T.O. in 1928;
- The rituals and degree workings of the Golden Dawn;
- The papers to do with The Lamp of Invisible Light;
- Memos, letters, coded telegrams, bank deals, and note books to do with the secret services of Britain, China, France, Russia (both Tsarist and Bolshevik), United States and

Egypt (under the Khedive[46] and later);
- Crowley's version of my, or our, first book ('Liber Fulgur');
- The annotated version of 'The Book of Desolation' in English;
- Some papers and maps, etc. which I refer to elsewhere in this book;
- Some ritual objects, e.g., a sanctuary lamp, a lavish book cover in wrought brass, tie-pins and odd bits of jewellery;
- The design and plans for a rather ambitious type of tantric dance which raises 'a ruinously powerful force'.

Nor is this all, but it's enough to be going on with.

Scandals and Shops

In Britain, the gutter press can shriek almost anything it wants. One comes across extraordinary headlines on the front pages of some: "The people cry: We are sick of the Monarchy!" Or yet again, "Does anybody trust this Minister?", and "Who the hell does this Churchman think he is?" All of them are tendentious, of course, and most of them are out to destroy Prince Charles.

It is the same, if not worse, in the rest of Europe and America. But they have no backing for their words. No one has actually asked the people what they think. When they thunder forth their statements, they are telling the people what they *ought* to think. They are not so much lying as looking at the truth from a particular angle. These are the men and women who change the world. And who pays their wages, one might well ask? Who are the grey men who sway the editors to go this way or that? What is the force that can wield such massive power in the contemporary world? I am not allowed to tell you, not right out. But this much I will say ... it isn't Saint George!

After them, we have those pathetic experts whose only claim to fame is that they've read all the available books. They remind me of the character, Otto, in that hilarious film, 'A Fish Called Wanda'. He had a complex about being stupid, so he ate Nietzsche at breakfast and forgot it all by suppertime. He did not grasp a solitary word but it made him feel good. He was doing what intelligent people were supposed to do, so he believed he

---

46. The 'viceroy' installed by the Turkish government (1867-1914).

was getting more like them. It did wonders for his poor, old ego ... but nothing else was very much changed at all. One could not really say that he was a student of philosophy, could one? Well neither can one call those other chaps students of the occult, however much they'd like it.

The world teems with this kind of failed scholar. They spend so much time in the library, their faces start to resemble old books. Whatever it is that they do, they delight in being seen doing it. One or two of them have been deeply impressed by a recent film on 'Dracula'. They have started to wear purple cloaks and weird rings on all eleven fingers. If it were possible, they'd come and go in puffs of smoke. They have to make do with a perfume that would paralyse a cat at a hundred yards.

But the others are a bit more subtle. They draw all eyes by a clever kind of modesty. They slip into that occult shop which looks like a Gipsy caravan that has been inverted. They glide in between the other folk like a shadow from a cartoon. They stand by the table that is piled high with packets of 'Welsh Sheep Turds', so fresh they are still steaming. They flit like a Sultan in disguise along the alleys of this strange 'occult bazaar'.

It is hard to find the shelf where Crowley's books are kept. One stumbles over girls in shawls trying to get 'the vibes'. One lifts and shifts gangling boys in a trance. They are all members of some joint illusion, like boy scouts, bikers, or people in church. There may be nothing to it but either you belong or you don't. They are all part of the same dream, sharing the same futile conspiracy – which is very good for business.

I went to a Voodoo shop in Paris. I was met by a beaming Negro whose skin glistened as if it had just been polished with shoe-wax. "What can I sell you, white boy?" he asked. I was not a boy and I felt that it was meant as a piece of effrontery or racial impertinence. So I looked at him steadily and, very slowly, I made my face go black. It was fascinating to watch his eyes grow in size. Like eggs that have broken in the frying-pan, there was a congealed yellow round the bulging white. He began to shake from top to toe.

"Can black skin grow pale?" I asked him.

He nodded and said, "We go grey, boss!"

"As if you had changed into dust?" I smiled very faintly and caressed his cheek. I held out my hand and showed it to him.

There was a heap of powder like cigarette ash. I let it sift through my fingers and vanish on the unswept floor.

"You are no longer a slave," I told him. "So throw away the fetters in your brain."

Except that it wasn't my voice. It was much deeper. Nor can I say that it was me who spoke. It was another being who had chosen to use me. The Negro knew who it was.

"*Obatala*," he murmured kissing the hem of my old, black raincoat. "*Obatala!*"[47]

The Ego

You realise how difficult it is to write about AC, without seeming to be pushing myself or my own ideas to the forefront. But be fair with me. I was and I am part of Aleister's plan. In spite of other people's doubts, I am the son he brought forth for a reason. I also belong to an earlier generation when views and values were different. It is hard to be the true English gentleman – modest and reserved – while at the same time filling my role as an occult Master. Needless to say, I do not behave like any recent Archbishop of Canterbury, nor like any Pope. What model could I use for my role?

The police have a school where they learn how to dodge Japanese tourists, and call all black people "sir" – even the women-folk. The cabin-staff of a large air company also go to school since they are responsible for the actual lives of their passengers. On the one hand, they are taught how to deal with terrorists. On the other, they learn what to do with people like me, the terror stricken. Come to that, priests and pastors spend years learning how to preach in that silly voice. They go to the same school as the chaps who make public announcements at large railway stations!

Come to that, the men who repair television sets are taught how to waste time, and then sell you a satellite dish or an x-ray machine. Last, but not least, there is your shop assistant. When the customer asks for one product, he or she is told to offer you alternatives. You ask for toilet paper, but you leave the shop with Christmas wrapping paper, sandpaper, and a dozen bags of confetti.

---

47. In the Yoruba language of Africa, this means 'the White God'.

41

I went to Tibet, but I found no trains to Agartha! I passed by Mongolia, and there were no signposts to Xanadu. I even dwelt in Jerusalem – Friday to Sunday are holy days, and Monday to Thursday are for rioting. I took one of those jolly, little holidays that are said to be of 'special interest'. From the bright, varied list, I chose the one that was called 'restoring antiques'. As things turned out, it proved to be a Keep-Fit course for old-folk.

"Anyway," I said to a French student, "it isn't easy being English and a Magician."

"Nuw," he replied, in a perfect imitation of the late Peter Sellers. "I serpose ze raern keels all ze ribbits."[48]

He never understood why I fell off the sofa and started threshing about on the floor. Nor did it help when he tried to guide the conversation on to "frantic yoga", which was "very interesting about him."

As I tire of telling folk: there are not all that many Teachers about. As a matter of fact, they are quite rare. It is even rarer for a Teacher to be succeeded by his own son. As far as one can tell, this has not happened before. In other words, I am a one-off. ("One uv wart?" I can almost hear that student asking.)

Luckily for me, Aleister did what he could to prepare me. As I said earlier, he did not have the right nor the authority to 'make' me a Master. He could only do his best and make an offering to the Gods.

"There is one great problem: for any would-be magician to overcome," he said to me one day. "It is how to divorce the 'Self' from 'Will'."

I had been studying occultism long enough by now to ask him why he didn't use the word 'ego' instead of 'self'.

"Ha," he chuckled as if I had hit upon one of the golden keys. "The Ego, as explained by Dr Freud, is only a small fraction of the whole 'self', whereas 'self' in all its grandeur embraces the entire cosmos."

48. "I suppose the rain kills all the rabbits."

7

GILTINE

The Goddess of death in Lithuania

Pro Patria

There is a practice common all over the world, and even more so in Europe. We raise our children to be heroes. Thus we coax them out of their childhood fears quickly. Consequently, most adults see 'Cowardice' as vile, and 'Courage' as a noble virtue. This is why most countries have medals and other awards for the fools who show blind valour. These are prizes for happy men who risk life and limb in killing 'the enemy'. You get nothing if you are simply reported as 'missing in battle'.

When these tributes are doled out, there is always the maximum of publicity. It is done to impress on dumb minds the concept of 'ideal conduct'. It may just act as a model for the timid ones. It tells them what's expected. When war is in season, then 'heroism' is in. At any other time we call it a 'death wish'. But the pressure can be softened once victory has been won.

Most civilized countries have a 'Tomb of the Unknown Warrior'. It might better be entitled 'The Tomb of Uncounted Millions', and it is indeed used as a symbolic resting place for all military dead from all times. A Cenotaph,[49] which somehow stands for the glory and greatness of a nation, is one thing. But a tomb that is both 'real' and 'symbolic' at the same time, becomes elevated to the status of a 'high place' or an 'altar'.[50]

49. A monument in Whitehall, London, which represents 'an empty tomb', or that of the resurrected Christ – or the hero who lives again.
50. It is also worth remembering that immolation, or the killing of a sacrifice, can be 'real' or 'symbolic' too. In particular, the offering of 'self' as a sexual 'victim' was always done within the precincts of a temple, or in the vicinity of a 'sacred tomb'. Indeed, it is part of a magician's training that he learn to set up just such a sacred place, and to keep it 'charged' with power.

In our films, our television and our books, a great deal of stress is put on selfless bravery and courage. Thus ordinary folk are made to feel guilty of their quite normal fears. So instead of letting them get rid of pressure, they keep it bottled up until, one day, there is a big explosion. Repressed fears can have a very bad effect on our mental stability.[51]

The reason for all this fuss about fear is easy to understand. First and foremost, fear is a natural and wholesome response to a threat since it helps us to cope with danger ... either by going berserk and attacking it, or by running in the opposite direction. One way or another we avoid the damage. Of course, all this was meant for a less clever, or even brainless creature so they would not blunder stupidly into harmful corners and be murdered.

Sadly, as Man evolved out of these older forms of life, he brought across some of their savage emotions. These relics of an old wildness can swamp out our mental effort. But, like a careful mother, nature insists that we keep them in our satchels, just in case. So quite often the negative emotion of fear can swamp the rational process. Yes, we could work out a more efficient response to danger, but our heritage throws us into panic instead.

Faced with looming danger, we either summon unusual powers (roused by the adrenalin produced by fear) or run away and save ourselves. Either way, we would *do* something. The result would then be that the fear is dissipated. We let off steam, so to speak. Having served its purpose, i.e., aroused action, it is then allowed to drain away. Worry is not action. Neither is anxiety. All they do is cause stress! Stress is only any good for raising the pH value of the skin, producing eczema. It also adds a heavy burden to the digestive system and the heart. Instead of dying quickly, you die slowly. It can take many years!

It helps if we understand our fears, so it's good to air them by talking to friends. If you prefer, you can talk to a doctor instead, but that is much more expensive, and he shows less intimate concern. In my opinion, anyone who works in the field of mental illness should be preceded by a boy waving a red-flag! Also, we have far too many of them and things would go much better if we rationed them out. Let us say: one for the Royal Family, one each

51. Here we can see society dividing menfolk up into hero-material and coward-stuff.

for all members of the government. Needless to say, the House of Commons should have new locks fitted quite quick. The noble Lords should be allowed to nibble the members, and vice versa.

Keys of Conduct

The world-wide stress on courage brought about the invention of 'codes of honour' and 'the look of things'. The result is that man is hyper-aware of public opinion, and more self conscious than any other beast. By letting members control one another, society keeps a strong grasp on all of us. An alien force then irons out our personal differences. We become uniform souls from the same mould.

Thus, since we feel that each other person is properly representative of all other people, we are afraid to be different. Both aware and unaware, we compare ourselves all the time to some inbuilt, abstract ideal of what we ought to be like. From this point on, we find it very difficult to be honest about what frightens us. Faced with danger, fear spurs the output of adrenalin. In its turn, this permits the muscles to generate energy, which we use to fight or flee.

No matter which, something is done that is latently helpful and the tension of fear relaxes. If we nullify the adrenalin we allay the symptoms of fear! (Perhaps Sir Francis Drake played bowls to *stifle* his fear of the Spanish armada and *not* because he was brave!)

But fear that is repressed and overly ridiculed, can cause *greater* damage than the object that aroused it. The simple, natural reaction is converted into something more dangerous than the event from which it was intended to protect us. Fear was meant to be a useful tool and not an implement of slavery.

Of all the fears that people suppress, none is more universal than the fear of death and dying. In the west we have created the situation where death is rarely mentioned. We don't talk about it because it is bad taste or clumsy. In some places it is rude to speak of toilets or functions of the body. If any allusion has to be made, then there are more seemly or elegant terms.

In Great Britain, for example, if a woman is widowed we speak of her as having 'lost' her husband. It does rather sound as if she is terribly careless and has left him in the car park. When someone has been ill for a long time and finally succumbs, we say he has 'passed on'. This all but conjures up a picture of their thumbing a lift on a common market lorry. One of the silliest things we say is: 'He buried his wife last week'. One is sorely tempted to ask: 'Was she dead?'

After a lifetime of avoiding the subject, and of trying not to think about it, it is no surprise that many people have an unnatural dread of death. This is shown in our penchant for horror films set in or around burial grounds, grave markers, coffins and the like. This is a fairly recent event. After all, in primeval times the vast majority of human beings never had the chance to die naturally. They never got to the end of their 'allotted span' because they were killed – by other human beings, by animals or by disasters.

Often they were mocked by their own tribe. (Beware the bourgeois who buys a house in the country! Check your back door is locked!) But in those distant days, there was no symbol to cause fear. Skulls and bones were just the bits one left in the pot! You can easily see why people developed no mystic dread – they had no time. They were busy chasing, or being chased by, the neighbours.

It wasn't all that bright to let yourself grow plump. Your extra weight gave you more 'mass appeal', and also slowed you down considerably. The ideal shape of the primeval era was something like that of modern day models – anything from thin to meatless! But for quite different reasons, of course. Fashion never entered into it. Just imagine, if our famous beauties went back in time, they'd be stuck in cages and stuffed with food! That's the way that French farmers make *foie gras*.

Thanatophobia
We dread death so much, we try not to think about it. Whenever we have a tiny ill, we wonder if it's the big one. A dizzy spell, headache, diarrhoea, or hiccups: we wonder "Is this it?" Death is important because it can't be avoided. Since it is the only door by which we leave, we ought to exit smoothly with hope. Perhaps a good preparation for death is the best start for the next world. Like the chrysalis which conceals a butterfly, our body is but a vehicle for the soul. You've had your ups and downs, mishaps and escapades, but now you near the end. The car lacks fuel, and so the spirit just steps out.

Perhaps you were fond of that old car. It may be a wrench to leave it behind. You haven't always been as good as you should be either. But you haven't been terribly bad. Why would the Gods allow remorse if it were futile? It doesn't come to make you sick. It comes to heal and make amends. Life has been made up of meetings and partings, hellos and goodbyes. It took time to learn to make friends. But nothing is being cut or destroyed. This act is drawing to a close, but the curtain will rise on the next. If there is any sense of loss, there is also a sense of joining.

Where you now go, we shall follow. We imagine it is a breaking off simply because we fear we shall not see you, touch you, hear you or speak to you. But our love is so much stronger than ordinary fear ... the division is due only to our being at different stages of development. You fly while we walk.

You are in the mountains while we stay on the plains. You go before but we shall follow and all shall be one because we remain one. You were not born to be harried by dread. Learn what is there, but do not guess at what you cannot know. Knowledge will come, and you shall not be blamed for ignorance. You sought to be one with your fellows. You sought love, home, and a place to put down the roots of awareness. You found it here, with us.

There is within us a certain kind of sorrow, true, but it is the sorrow of children who do not understand why father or mother must leave them for a while. But just as those children smile with joy when the day's end (evening) brings their loved one's return – so we shall all be reunited at the eventide of life.

Fear not that you have or have not fulfilled this or that recipe or formula ... that you have not recited this or that prayer ... that you have not received this or that sacrament. God is above the rules and dogmas of men and their religions, and God can see men's hearts more clearly than men can rumble their own infants. Your heavenly father knows you better than you know yourself.

Don't be afraid that you may not have expressed to God what you wished in your soul to convey to him. Your heart sings it. Your soul chants it. Our love confirms it. Trust. Trust now. It has not been in vain. It was all for a purpose. You tried, you did your best. The past is past. Yesterday can *not* be recalled and changed. All that is needed is the will to make a better today so that the world's tomorrow shall be closer to success.

The baby is disturbed to be born but born it must be for it's time has come. So the human soul shrinks from dying, yet die it must when it's time has come. The spark of life is kindled in the cave within the side of the mountain ... and to the sides of that mountain we must all return. Our childhood over, we must go onward and upward. Let your soul be clothed in serenity now. Let your spirit shine with peace. You have worked in the fields and you have earned your rest. The worry is over. Let your going be seemly.

The soul is always concerned to leave this world in familiar surroundings. This is because home and family were the port from which we started out. It helps the spirit to be beside the faces one has loved. This assures us that the nature of the bond is changing, but not being broken. The love that was tested in life, will provide an enduring truth in death.

Second Ordeal
To a very great extent, fear of death is a mixture of two other things: (a) a fear of the unknown, and (b) a fear of being called to account. Well this much is fairly certain: the possible judgement that may be passed will be based on the life that you led. How much of it was spent on being natural, and how much was wasted on living up to the public model? Did you try to be happy? Or did you try to earn approval? Other people are very fond of passing their verdict but God did not appoint them as jurors.

Because you do have this fear of dying, you attach very great importance on finding the very best of Teachers. At first glance, there are hundreds of them about. Which of them dare you let yourself listen to? Here you have to face facts. You have a sceptical mind. You are going to doubt all of them. Even if, eventually, you register for lessons with one of them, a part of you'll be dubious to your dying day. You will never be able totally to believe that any of them is up to it.

Of course, you can fall back on the notion of full spiritual obedience. It is what all monks and nuns have done. You entrust the welfare of your soul to someone willing to accept it, e.g., a Prior, an abbess or a mother superior. In effect, you submit your will to that of God. But try as you might, there are bound to be small moments of rebellion. Your own Will never ceases to whisper. "Does he know what he's doing? Can I rely on him? How can I be sure that he is genuine?"

It is very difficult to accept that the teachings of the world throughout all ages represent the sum total of living knowledge. Yet they aim to coach the growing 'self' into a maturity that is enough to claim its heritage. Each of us has the right to personal access to truth. But to reach this point, we must shake off the rebukes of the nursery and the quarrels of our childhood. Just as each puppy must confront its first rat, so each schoolboy must struggle with the monsters in his mind.

You must also realize that what you discover may be a truth that applies only to this world. You will think it is very important and guard it along with your treasures. But it may be a burden. You may be carrying rotten apples on your holy quest. They will infect anything else you come across. Their blight will reach your heart. But, oh, it is all but impossible to throw away these dear but futile vanities. Man would insist on taking salt to the sea. Who can explain to him that his values are wrong? It would be like telling a farmer that he had scattered the wrong seed.

"Do you expect me to walk along the furrows picking it all up?" he would ask in disbelief.

"No," the Teacher must answer. "I suggest that you change your ground."

You should not worry about *which* of the various schools of truth might be the most important. I advise you, instead, to find out why you are here.

Oh yes! Having mentioned 'The Second Step', you will probably want to know about the one that precedes it. That is very easy to explain. But, I'm afraid, it is even harder to master. 'The First Step' consists of not being afraid of your own self.

8
PETBE

*An old Egyptian God of Retaliation and that aspect of death that is
to do with settling accounts*

Cemeteries
Near the heart of Paris is the cemetery of Père Lachaise. It is
named after a priest who was Confessor to the King. His
house and garden were once on this land. Frenchman or tourist,
you must visit this cemetery. It has its own grandeur, and its
secrets.

Not only the French are buried here. One striking tomb is that
of Oscar Wilde. There are always a few fresh flowers. But there
are so many celebrities, you can buy a special 'map' at the gate. It
includes a list of poets, painters, singers, actors and well known
courtesans. Schools often bring their classes here.

When Aleister first took me there, in 1938,[52] he walked through
the gates with an exuberant air. "Thank you," he flapped his map
in an attendant's face. "I've already get one!"

"How long have you had it?" I asked.

"Almost twenty years," he said.

"But there must have been lots of funerals since then."

He gave me a frown. "I have a propelling pencil!"

Despite his air, Crowley was not a snob. When he chose to ape
some one, his copy was more real than the model. As we entered
Père Lachaise, he became a funeral director. I was his lad. No one
noticed how small I was to be learning such a trade. Along one of
the avenues, we met an elderly lady, draped in dignity and
hauteur. Aleister tilted his head.

---

52. See Chapter 9, Epona.

"About the same height, eh, Jacot?"[53] He doffed his hat and gave a little bow. "Would madame be so kind ... ? Her shadow is of enormous help."

"*Vas te taper la veuve Poignet!*"[54] she spat coarsely, and walked into the arms of a stone angel. It quite made my father's day.

Père Lachaise is a museum of culture too, for the style of the tombs changes according to date. You can see neo-gothic, and art nouveau, or even art deco. There are fine pieces of sculpture and there are ghastly ones. In the same vein, there are many types of grave. They range from the small stone with a number, to mortuary palaces. Some of them are so grand, you almost expect to hear the rehearsal for an opera. "Here lies a great person," this one seems to say. "Here lies a nobody", sigh a dozen others.

There is no space *between* the tombs. Strange how this makes one uneasy. You cannot skirt round one grave to reach another unless you step on one. If you have always been taught to respect the dead, this makes you shudder. But custom bows to necessity. Land for burial has always been scarce in Paris. In Père Lachaise, a plot is paid for in gold ... and a plot is all you get. Not a millimetre more. When shock and grief are over, the family wonder do they really need a footpath round the grave? No-one is going to hold a party. You have to draw the line somewhere. So that is how they leave it, with an invisible boundary.

The most common tomb is your 'mini chapel'. If they were a wee bit cleaner, they'd look like a bathing hut, or a telephone kiosk. It is bad when it's raining. It's even worse with a mist in the air. It looks like a deserted bus station with thousands of empty shelters. They are as wide and as long as the grave which they cap. They have tiny windows, an iron grille and a doll-size altar with some broken, ceramic flowers.

The floor of a chapel is the lid of a hole which may be very deep. The coffins have been lowered down to the 'bottom'. Then each one has been given a 'floor' to support the next. One may think of them as a tottering tower of cigar boxes. One prays that no-one did any shoddy work. One walks with great care. Then

53. This is the Parisian argot for something like 'dick-head'.
54. This says, "Go and treat yourself to the five-fingered widow!" This means 'Go have a wank,' or 'Fuck off!' The exact nuance depends on the face, and the hand gesture, made at the time of speaking.

you look again at the lack of space between the graves and you realize that the whole damned cemetery must sag. The 'ground' is as flimsy as plastic foam. One 'big' funeral – one bus-load of Japanese ...

Empty Graves

Death can come very suddenly. But in view of the speed, a funeral director may be faced with a technical problem. When he opens the tomb, several floors have indeed collapsed, or else they rushed the previous burial and used a layer of solid concrete! You can see the snag. One can't use pneumatic drills at a funeral. It has a bad effect on the choirboys. So for just such a dilemma, a good firm owns a 'temporary grave'. The corpse just lodges there for a week or two. But this is not a hole with a lid on. There is a workshop down there. In the old days, they unscrewed the silver fixtures.

The funeral takes place when the family wishes, but when the coffin is lowered, two aides receive it on a trolley. Mourners do their thing – scatter earth, splash holy water or, if cameras are present, chuck in a rose. Then the wet and muddy workers wheel the coffin into a small, adjacent workshop which now functions as a 'waiting room'. The grave will be hidden by the flowers. All in good time, when the true grave is ready, the coffin will be moved.

Some of these 'temporary graves' date back to the opening of the cemetery. If you'll pardon the pun, many firms of funeral directors have since died out. So their 'false tombs' have also been forgotten. But this doesn't seem to make much difference, for they are still well tended. There are fresh flowers at Christmas, Easter and the Feast of All Souls. Since there is not, nor ever was, anyone inside, this is very strange.

Paris is short of graves. Each year therefore she claims back those that seem destitute. One may 'buy' a plot for perpetuity, for fifty years, or even less, but after a man's death – he is not remembered when his children have also died. After fifty years, no one cares – least of all the dead man. So the bones are dug up and placed in an 'ossuary'. In Père Lachaise, this is a fine work of art; where draped figures 'walk away' into a dark tunnel.

But the law says that a tomb bought 'in perpetuity' may not be opened as long as it is visited. This means flowers, cleaning, or the sight of someone paying respects. Ownership of the false tombs is preserved by people being paid 'to do the necessary'. They put flowers there. They kneel at the graveside. They ask the porters to show them the way. Simple! Who goes to these lengths? Who has a use for an empty grave? The answer is: Black Magicians.

The same things happens at Highgate cemetery in London, and other spots in Europe and America. Check our your old newspapers. Every few years, there is a 'ghastly scandal' in a burial ground. Graves are profaned, bones are scattered, and 'obscene' symbols have been daubed on the stones. After a short spurt of interest, everyone forgets. The crime is put in a file with the others. The point is though, there *are* many others. Oh yes. Evil is being worshipped in those places that the community thinks are sacred. Where sleep our dead – the devils are dancing.

I told you[55] how Aleister let me watch a comic 'Black Mass'. It was funny because of the people's gravity and lack of know-how. It was also AC's wicked sense of humour. But the nature of the event was evil. The gathering was seeking the help of Satan. The odd thing is: my story upset some Crowley fans who like to think of Crowley as a Black Magician. They argue with my version of things even though I was there. They do not grasp what Crowley was about. Granted, he rarely expressed himself in simple language. But he was trying to hide the fact that he hadn't much to say.

Let me quote from an old book:[56]

"Crowley was the last disciple of the 'Satanic' Gnostics ... *It was the theology of knowledge of the conflict of opposites, and the belief that a knowledge of evil was necessary to achieve final illumination ...* Whether they correspond to objective realities or not, *the dualistic concept in one form or another has so dominated man's intellectual and moral horizons that it appears to be fundamental to his thinking and experience.*" (My italics.)

The style is typical of its time. AC had been dead for seven years. But the writer should never have called him the last of anything; he was merely 'the most recent'. I do not agree with the statement, but it edges closer to the truth.

---

55. 'The Secrets of Aleister Crowley', Diamond Books, 1991, Chapter 11.
56. 'The Satanic Mass', H.T.F. Rhodes, Rider, 1954.

Om Mane Padme Hum

> All that is visible, clings to the invisible,
> the audible to the inaudible,
> the tangible to the intangible:
> Perhaps the thinkable to the unthinkable.
>
> (Novalis)

In Buddhist symbolism, the Knower becomes one with that which he knows. He and his knowledge are united for all time. One starts to know at a very early age – much younger than is the opinion among current experts. So, if and when a soul begins to know Truth, he already knows a great deal of Untruth. If he knows both things, then they cancel each other out and the Knower is less than nothing. But if the Knower first makes room for Truth, by throwing the Untruth into the realm of Unknown, then he will not only see the Truth – he will apprehend it. He will make it part of himself.

These concepts are hard to grasp. The mind tries to take hold of them but they are as slippy and as elusive as eels. The great gurus of India and Tibet try to give their students access to the meanings of these words by the use of mantras. That is to say: they make use of magical sound. In the 'Surangama Sutra'[57] the Buddha takes a silk scarf and ties a knot in it. When asked what he sees, Ananda replies: "A silk scarf with a single knot in it." The Buddha then ties a second knot, a third knot, and so on until there are six knots. Each time Ananda gives the same answer, simply giving the number of knots. "Ah," said the Buddha, "but each knot was tied in another way, and you did not notice that."

This lesson was meant to explain a simple point. If anyone pretends to be a top-notch yogi who has released the higher chakras then he is a fool. He has not yet untied the lower ones. To know how to untie any knot, one must first know how that knot was tied. Otherwise, one takes the grave risk of making the knot even tighter and more complex.

Crowley was no stranger to Buddhism or to Tantrism. We must not forget that two of his closest friends, Alan Bennet and Gerald

---

57. In 'A Buddhist Bible', translated by Bhikshu Wai-tao and Dwight Goddard, 1938, reprints Harrap 1957.

Yorke, became Buddhists either because of, or in spite of, Master Therion's influence. What is true is that AC applied a very similar principle to the study of life and used it for climbing the path toward 'total integrity'. If you recall, this was also the aim of the Cathar 'Perfecti'. It is often called entelechy – i.e., making real that which is one's potential.

Now death is the logical corollary of life. That mouth of the ossuary at Père Lachaise is not a devourer of the dead but a gateway through which all pass. But the dead may need guidance to recognize this as a stairway and not the edge of a Roman precipice.[58]

The practice of 'Graveyard Magic' means that someone in 'this' world is trying to capture the energies of 'that' world for private use. If White Magic were ever practised in a graveyard, it would be to help 'lost souls' find their way again. In order to achieve this latter goal, a magician must know what 'death' is. In this respect, it is terribly significant that the French refer to orgasm as "the little death."

Before anyone leaps yet again for the label "obsessed with sex", they might care to illumine their ignorance about Tantrism. The word 'Tantra' relates to the idea of 'weaving', and carries with it the sense of everything in the cosmos being somehow linked. Thus, those actions carried out in body, speech or thought can have mystical effects. They generate karma from human will and empower the Magician (or *sadhaka*) to bend the dynamic forces of the cosmos to his own purposes.[59]

Rounding Off
What is 'thinkable' in a graveyard, is that the dead have gone to rest. What is 'unthinkable' is that they may come back. Just as a mother gives birth, the outcome of one magical deed, so we may start a second birth, as the outcome of another. I will give you a whopping clue. In English, cardinal numbers from one to a million are built with words from the original tongue. The same applies to all the ordinal numbers ... except one, *'the number that does not fit'*. This is 'second'. It should be *'other'*.

58. Throwing people off a cliff was a common method of execution in ancient Rome.
59. cf H. von Glasenapp, 'Die Entstehung des Vajrayana', Zeitschrift der Deutschen Morgenlandischen Gesellschaft. Leipzig 1936.

Do not forget that 'other' can have a variant sense, i.e., the alternate or proxy. One can talk about the 'other' king, or the 'other' ritual. One can also have 'other' motives, and one's words can have 'other' meanings. Do you glimpse what might be meant by *my other self, the other world, a second coming* and *otherwise?*

Now what I said about 'black magic' and 'spoiling of tombs' are not necessarily connected. Occult hoodlums will do anything to let loose their contempt for the system, but don't be misled by their antics. Bad publicity may be used to draw attention from *other* things. Old churches and old cemeteries were often built on pagan sites. They tried to lure the 'sheep' from one sanctuary into the other. There are 'sacred spots' near many religious monuments, and some are more potent than others. Père Lachaise is a fairly 'new' cemetery, but there was a pagan site in the priest's garden. There is such a spot in Brookwood Cemetery in Surrey, south of London.[60]

These holy sites often took the form of 'grottoes' or 'caves'. To people long ago, they were an 'omphalos', the 'navel' of the Great Earth. They were therefore a means of contact with power. When the need arose, one disguised them as 'graves'. They were the portals to the 'other world' and on their threshold a would-be Druid got ready to visit the Land of the Dead. These portals still exist. They were there before the druids came. This explains why one can meet a genteel lady who speaks like a slut. It is why one finds the remnants of fires, sacred meals, and a 'dosser's squat'.

In many parts of Celtic Europe, the burial grounds are less like resting places and more like lobbies. One must look for marks. If one searches without authority, then one is pixie-led[61] or made mad. Please do not go trooping there in droves. Do not be slave to your impulses. Don't be magical 'tourists' who play such silly games. Before you move, answer this question. Why did AC keep the map for twenty years? I still have it, by the way.

---

60. It even had a special railway line built to 'ease the traffic'.
61. An ancient idea still exists that human beings can be led astray, or made to lose their way, by the 'fairies' or 'the little ones' – i.e., the spirits of nature.

9

EPONA

The name of a goddess meaning 'big mare' who was sacred to a fertility cult

First Stop

"Many things can happen to one in France," declared AC, "and most of them are terribly nice." His eyes twinkled like the lights on a Christmas tree. "And it is critical for your education that you see France before you are very much older."

In 1938, he instructed my mother on how she could arrange for my absence from school. He then managed to get my name included on his passport,[62] and off we went to France. I was then in my eighth year and he had already started to teach me magic. But I was still at junior school, and I hadn't yet begun to learn the French language. The outcome was that village names meant little to me, even if I heard them correctly. As for people, even when I was presented, I could only pick up whatever Crowley called them himself.

Nowadays, it would be easy to 'guess' at the slender gaps in my memory. But that would not be fair. For example, if I recall a name that sounded like "Moh Budge", it is tempting to imagine it was the town Maubeuge. But I can't be sure. I had better not be tempted and leave any 'help' to people who perhaps live in the areas I seem to mention. Better still if they were still alive. Do they remember "Luh grant Onglay" and his "jurn feese".[63] I would love to hear from you.

We went to a town where one could watch women sitting in doorways or close to windows working on lace. They had small

---

62. How convenient it would be if that document still existed! But he had several passports in his possession, many of them from different countries.

63. Le grand Anglais et son jeune fils.

cushions on their laps, that were stuck with pins. Their fingers worked like an organist attacking a Bach Toccata and Fugue, too fast for me to see what they did. I remember a board where a series of small, round pieces of lace were displayed. They were identical except that each had the word 'mother' in a different tongue. I didn't know this, but Aleister showed me. Being from Yorkshire, I found the German word *'mudder'* was notably easy to hear and repeat correctly.

I used to think that this town was called "Bovay". There were no motorways in those days, and the ancient town of Beauvais did lie on one of the major routes from the channel ports to Paris. However, there doesn't seem to be any linkage between this town and the lace that is clear in my mind. Could it be that we just passed through Beauvais? Was it our next stop? Or did I just mistake what I heard?

We stayed at a largish house, and I was startled to find that the upper floor had an outside passage. The roof of the house covered it, of course, yet this was the only way of getting from one room to another. In the evening we went to a meeting in what I took to be a cellar or a cave. The owner of the house was called Mister "Var-gin-co" and he said that this was once a cellar used for wine. Everything had been killed off by "bronchitis",[64] which was a ruinous disease, and since this was a "trivial" zone, they had never started again. They may have done so now, of course. We held a ritual during the night. The object was "to bring back strength to the sep".[65]

The next morning we used a public bus to go and see a great cathedral. I had already seen Canterbury cathedral in the company of AC and grandad, but this one did not seem to be as big. I remember being totally paralysed by fear when they showed me a real body inside a glass case. Whatever it was they were telling me, I kept my eyes fixed on the body's chest to see if it was breathing. I think it very likely that they told me whose body it was but I didn't register a thing. I'm not quite sure, but I have the impression that it was dressed in red.[66]

---

64. Botrytis, or grape-rot.
65. I now know that 'cep' is the French word for the root of the vine.
66. This could be 'back projection' and unreliable. I have seen other reliquaries containing the bodies of martyrs, and they were dressed in red.

Second Stop

We continued our journey by bus, but got off at some lonely spot in the wild outlands. A man with a pony and trap was waiting for us, and I found the rest of our journey quite special. He lived at a farm but on the upper floor. The ground floor was for animals and workers. His wife, mother and sons ate with us. The young men looked enormous to me, and they wore wooden clogs or 'sabows'. None of them was married. The mother said she'd stop feeding them and hunger might kindle their fires.

Before twilight we had enough time left to visit some ancient ruins that were close by. They were not standing stones or menhirs, but actual buildings that had fallen. One could see the remains of an arch and of a staircase – but there was no wood at all in the structure. Either it had rotted away, or it had been ripped out to be used as fuel, many years previously.

That evening, after supper, we went to a big barn and crowds of people were waiting. Each person, or so it seemed, wanted a private word with AC. They formed a sort of queue by sitting on benches along the walls on one side. Crowley sat at the other side, privately, almost like a priest hearing penitents. The odd thing was that he made me sit some ten feet away from him, facing an empty chair. Whenever the person he spoke to was blonde, he sent him along to me.

Now I emphasize again that I spoke no French, and none of these people spoke any English. I don't know how we overcame this problem but we conversed quite easily and I cannot for the life of me remember how. It would be a handy point at which to introduce one more little miracle. I dare say it would enliven my story and increase the possibility of a film being made. But, I'm sorry. If anything untoward had taken place, I think it would have stuck in my mind. These blonde people just studied my eyes and spoke. I understood what they said and gave them my reply. I could see that they grasped what I said too.

In my first book,[67] I discussed the great Ritual that took place near to the Rollright Stones when I was made an Initiate. If you remember, at one point, I was brought face to face with an amazing 'twin' with golden hair. Now that was to happen six years later, when I had reached the age of fourteen! I can not

---

67. 'The Secrets of Aleister Crowley'.

explain why AC did all this. I have often wondered if he might have been preparing me in some way. Afterward, it did cross my mind to ask if I wasn't being implanted with some type of 'Aryan' leaning.

But quite recently, my mother came out with one of her own flashes of insight. She is now in her mid-eighties, but she has a lively memory. She told me something that took place so long ago that it totally slipped my mind. When I was four, and we still lived with Len Standish, my playmate died of tuberculosis and I wept for weeks. She has kept a small, faded photo of him. He has curly blond hair and eyes as blue as centaury.[68]

Now I can't say for certain if this helps or not. I don't know how much it means, if it means anything at all. In a way, I suppose there might be some connexion with his abiding spirit – i.e., that part of him which goes on from one rebirth to another. But equally, we might be speaking of some deep, forgotten scar in my own psyche. I do not know, and that is being honest. I really do not know. I keep that photo with great care, but try as I might, I have no conscious memory of him.

Fontainebleau

Yes, to my small ears, this sounded like 'Fountain Blue', but I don't think there is any room for mistake. For one thing, he took me to see a huge house or a palace, where I was totally bored. He was a little annoyed by my lack of interest, and told me so.

"Just imagine what it must have been like – actually to have lived here," he said.

I tried. "It echoes too much," I replied. "I'd have been scared." I looked at a woman in costume gliding across the shining floor. She went out through a closed door. "Besides," I gulped, "there are ghosts."

He nodded affably. "France is full of ghosts," he said. "They had a fine old time making them!"[69]

In the early evening, at the modest hotel at which we were staying, we had a visit from a Mister 'Good-chef.' He greeted AC by flinging his arms around him and holding on for a very long time. I remember hoping that he would not do the same to

---

68. Or the common cornflower.
69. I had not then heard mention of the French Revolution and the Reign of Terror. But I assume this is what he was referring to.

me. Instead he lifted me up and held me level with his eyes. They seemed black, like pieces of coal stuck on to the face of a snowman. He also had a big moustache.

"So," he said slowly, "This is the one?" I felt like a piece of art-work being examined by an expert.

"Amado," AC said in clear, precise English, "This is my old friend, your uncle Gor-gee." Both g's were hard. For a moment I thought he'd said "Korky," who was a cat in my weekly comic book. In fact, of course, it was Gyorgi – the Russian mystic known as Gurdjieff.[70]

The man then embraced me with a couple of big, wet kisses and I wrinkled my nose because his breath smelled. He was quite amused at this and told me it was garlic. This meant nothing at all to me. I had never heard of it. I didn't read 'Dracula' until I was twelve years old. I simply assumed it was some sort of French perfume, or a medicine for bad teeth.

When Gor-gee asked if he could dress me up, AC grinned and agreed. I was put into a long, creamy coloured coat that reached my boots, and they put a tall red hat on my head. It was in fact an authentic costume for a dervish, but I can only guess it had been made especially for me. I have no idea if the Dervishes would usually have these garments in kids' sizes.

"Turn!" ordered Gor-gee. I turned. "Again!" he snapped. I turned again. And he kept on ordering me to turn, time and time again, and started saying "Faster, faster!"

I had to stretch my arms out in order to adjust my balance, but in no time at all I discovered the knack. The long skirts of the heavy coat flew out by centrifugal force and acted as a species of gyroscope. I noticed that my feet were tapping out a rhythm and my eyes did not fix on a single point, as would a dancer's.

Round and round I went. I felt a heavy dull sensation on my ears as if I'd gone deaf suddenly ... and then the music started. I did not recognize the rhythm nor the timing. It sounded like flutes, drums and the caterwaul of an untuned violin. I realized I was floating. I was rising up in the air. I heard voices. I saw faces. And there descended on me a peace that I can not convey with words.

70. We did not visit Gurdjieff's house, Le Chateau de Prieure, which AC had helped to find. cf; 'The Riddles ...', Chapter 16.

61

I must have fainted, or fallen asleep. When I awoke I was sprawling in a huge winged chair. AC and Gor-gee were talking softly but earnestly, and they went on for a very long time. I tried sending out hints by squirming in my chair. I even slid off the seat and stretched out on the carpet. It made no difference at all and I fell asleep again. This time I woke up suddenly, feeling very guilty. The two of them were staring at me fixedly.

"Beg pardon," I said, feeling that I had been very rude. I climbed back into the big chair.

"No," said Gor-gee. "Do not be sorry."

He bowed his head and seemed to be unutterably sad. I was a little bit alarmed. I glanced at AC, and he was every bit as dejected. "What did I do?" I whispered with fear.

"You told us when the war is due."

"Oh dear," I said, thinking it was wrong.

Gor-gee managed a tight little smile and pulled me against his coat. "You told us about a special bomb and how many it will cause to die."

I was so shocked I don't recall very much more. My guess is that this is when they made plans for Gor-gee's flight to England just before warfare came to France. As I said in my first book, we met him several times during the war, when he was lodged at Frinton-on-Sea.

Pipe-Dreams

I am going to quote some words that fell direct from Crowley's mouth. Up to now, of course, I have tried to work these examples into snatches of normal conversation, but that isn't possible this time. What he told me was too profound for any literary licence. Indeed, I am sad enough that I cannot vouch that everything I say is one hundred per cent accurate. I don't dare to guarantee that each and every word is authentic, either. It wasn't my father's choice of words that hit me hardest, but their meaning. I have done my best to piece it all together again and I hope that you will find it as poetic and poignant as I do. Do please remember that I am going back some fifty years. I am quoting as precisely as I can manage. Here goes:

– Life goes quicker than expected. We grow old in a state of surprise. Then we find a souvenir that brings it all back. It was behind a drawer or lost in a trunk. A letter, a photo, a reminder of a dream that did not come true. Our legs go weak. We fumble for a seat. "Fancy that," we gasp, midway between a whisper and a sigh. A tiny wetness dampens our eye.

- That is youth! Blazing plans one day, cold embers the next. The days drag like a funeral past your gates and then, too soon, it is all half ended. That is the secret in an old woman's eyes. How silly we are. How pointless it was. Both tears and dew have dried. We are born to be bygones.

- Guilt can blind us to the good we did. We think we have lost. We don't see how we could win. How sad to grow old with no hope. We wrinkle like shelves of apples. We grow smaller like babies? Dreams are not truth, but their light can show us truth. Peace, like sleep, has been won.

- Like a diamond, life needs space to be perfect. But space and not emptiness; life and not a void. Are you one of those dustbins that dare not be emptied? Are you a bud that refuses to flower on manure?

- You want to do better? You would, if you stopped talking.

- The forces of evil know something you don't. They take you to a carnival and get you drunk. That is why you made life's most vital choices – with the eye of a child.

- Live, or drop of inertia! Bang your head, beat your breast, howl your defiance. Rock the boat, don't let it drift. Hoist a sail, swing the wheel. Take a new Pilot on board.

I have tried to reproduce his words, and it helps to imagine him speaking them. There is a lot more in these few stanzas. One last thing: when we went to Chartres to meet 'the resistance,' AC's code-name was 'snowdrop.'

10

ULL

A German God concerned with administration and justice

Public Disquiet

"France's great problem is her bureaucracy!" So said Aleister.
"They should shoot one civil servant in five." On the whole, he
liked the French people. He felt very happy in their company. But
he could not see why they let so many officials live. "Could they
not make a stew?" he would ask? But while foreigners suffer – it
is the French people themselves who choke on red-tape. Illegal
migrants think of France as paradise, but the average civil servant
can make it hell. They have a genius for losing documents. They
can lose anything. When the police were charged with selling
drugs, they lost an entire room where the evidence was kept! "Ah
well," sighed Aleister. "You let them win Liberty. Then you stop
them using it!"

Every clerk feels he is head of the Seventh Empire. It never
occurs to them that they are all puppets, whose strings are being
pulled by *secret chiefs*. I don't say there is a link, but the head of
the Freemasons used to be the brother of President Mitterand![71]
Look at the archive from the revolution on; you'll see a fine array
of Masonic icons. Furthermore, a clumsy system can be helpful to
a chosen few. Kafka knew a thing or two!

Most Freemasons think there are only three degrees of
member: Entered Apprentice, Fellow Craft, and Master Mason.
No one tells them about the secret part, called 'The Ancient and
Accepted Rite of the 33rd Degree.' Even the British Royal Family
is ignorant. Now within this tangle, the eighteenth degree has an
exotic title: *Sovereign Prince Rose Croix of Heredom*.[72] In short, a

71. Stephen Knight, ibid.
72. Stephen Knight, ibid.

council of five Masons oversees The Rose Croix. It's no good asking them – they are all sworn to silence.

It is useful to recall that Pius XII signed 'an understanding' with Hitler. Each agreed to respect the property and personnel of the other. Jean Moulin, the French patriot, was betrayed in the city of Lyons – where the Germans found thousands of civil servants willing to work for them. Who helped Klaus Barbie to evade capture for forty years? Who hid other war criminals and traitors? The story leaves a nasty taste in the mouth.

It is a French tradition that all blame delegates down, while all praise climbs up. So some go skiing, as others block the roads with tractors. You can always tell which side is winning – the police join them. Everyone shoots at everyone else, but especially tourists. In the great lorry-strike of 1992, the score was one Dane, three Dutch and a brace of Swiss.

The civil servant is deeply detested and he doesn't much like himself. He has a job for life and a guaranteed pension. Go to a post office and you'll see the result. You wait so long, your passport runs out. But one breath of complaint and BANG! The shutter comes down like a guillotine. "One has to answer nature," she says sweetly. The time she's gone, she could have struck oil.

It is very rare to catch a civil servant working. They are plugged in to telephones like saline drips. They study files, which are upside down. They gaze at empty computer screens. One actually died. No one knew till a dog ran off with him. Luckily it was a French poodle.

As to the Revolution ... it isn't over! It breaks out again from time to time, usually on a nice week-end. Let tourists take note: if hotels are cheaper around the Bastille, there's a good reason. You may never get there. You will be sucked into a good old riot. The police will thump you, hose you down, and lock you up. This could be the holiday you'll never forget.

Solidarity

When the French do things they do not do them by halves. Too many British sheep? – burn them alive. Too much English fish? – shoot the Royal Navy. No foot shuffling here. None of this muttering under your breath. A Frenchman has this gift of going temporarily berserk. He climbs lamp-posts and pees on you. He rips up paving stones and wangs them about like frisbees. Keep your eyes peeled. They measure their riots on the Richter Scale! Cars go zoom past third floor windows. When the statues start to run ... join them.

If you see men in padded suits, wielding shields, and battering every head in sight – do not ask for the Metro. This is not your British Bobby. Above all, forget about cricket, and do not try to field smoking tins of Coca-cola. They are tear-gas bombs.

After the Revolution, they gave new names to the months of the year. These were then assigned to various classes of workers so they would not all strike at the same time. The docks and airports get Easter and Christmas. The teachers get June, just when school exams take place. Nurses and doctors get November, in time for the annual 'flu epidemic. While gas and electric go for January, the first and the coldest month of the year. Any good travel agent can supply you with a copy of the official strike agenda.

Farmers are the odd men out. They strike when they feel like it. The most popular weapon is a loaded lorry of pig shit, rotten cabbages, or ravaging herds of berserk sheep. The radio gives bulletins telling you where not to drive. There is also a network of escape routes called, oddly enough, 'bison fuité'. It means 'the run-away buffalo'![73] I think this is an example of Gallic wit.

To come back to the civil service: there is a code of conduct. They are paid to give you a hard time. The basic method is as delicate as that of a crow ripping up a worm. Any clerk can ask for the signature of your last teacher, even if he's dead. He can dispatch you to an address on the twelfth floor of a building that vanished during the War. He can invoke geology if he wants, or order a seismic survey of your house. In brief: he has got you by the short and curlies!

Aleister said it was all to do with rubber stamps. "Phallic symbols, you see! Put two in his hand and you provoke his virility." I speak from bitter experience. I have had to face these things. Ask your local Mayor for a Visitor's Permit. Try to register a used car. Go with a friend to give notice of a birth. Your hair will also turn grey. When you go mad you move to Switzerland where they are not likely to notice.

---

73. To be truthful, these are 'secondary routes' which help one avoid the spectacular tail-backs that occur at holiday times.

Don't argue with a civil servant. Never say he's wrong. Even if he is hideously deformed, pretend you're in love. Polish his shoes and dust his desk. Drop a few banknotes you have freshly ironed. Titivate his hair or, if he's bald, massage his scalp. If it's a woman, stare at her breasts. If it's a man, stare at his crotch with envy. If he likes boys, give him your nephew. If he's small, bend your knees. If you're handsome, dot your face with a pencil.

Then, when you've got what you want, say he's a swine. Tell him he speaks French quite well for someone with his handicap. Ask him what time he finishes work and leer. Ask him what model of car he drives, and grin. Slip a rubber scorpion in his pocket or better still, a live one. It will make you feel better.

As I write, there is turmoil in Russia. Civil war brings ruin to some of the smaller states. Fascism has awakened from its long sleep in Germany. In the Near East as well as Europe, Islamic tensions bubble. Mark my words: blood will flow in the streets of western cities. But you don't need crystal balls to foresee that France will not do badly. Or I should say – some folk will survive even if the rest are knocked off. They have links, you see.

Good and Bad points
The Mafia has an annual income that beats many states in the European Community. Who gains *most* from the Common Market? Not the common people, that's for sure. Why are we told to put land to rest and stop producing food, when millions of people are starving elsewhere? Who makes money out of each and every disaster? Are they the same people who set up wars? Who are the leeches who drain off the billions that are missing in Europe?

Are the poor less poor? Are the rich less rich? Is war less likely now? Some of you will scoff. Let the police take their names. Others will call me naive. Don't forget who they are. We have a saying in Britain: "the Devil takes care of his own!" He is doing so in Europe, isn't he?

I must be careful what I say. The French are so charming and also so very sensitive. They know it and they are proud of it. One could never accuse them of being too modest. They enjoy life to the maximum and their welcome knows no bounds. How silly it would be to spoil it all by being coy. "It is your island," they say of Great Britain. "You live wiz rain and zat 'orrible food. You expect ze worst and take umbrellas to ze Cote d'Azur! Oh yes, you 'ave class. But we French 'ave ze charm."

But one meets Frenchmen with no charm, just as one meets English who lack class. But, despite the long history of war between our two countries, I think we probably like each other. Even so, the 'Entente Cordiale'[74] is dead.

This is the way that the Masonic intrigue worked in France. They sold the French the concept of 'grandeur'. They held 'glory' in front of their eyes. They told her lies about her future role in the destiny of nations. They study one's weak points, you see. Notice what they did with Louis XIV. Just look how they used Napoleon! And what about the Maginot Line? They said it could not be crossed. But the Bosch just strolled across it, as if someone had given them the plans. And why did the French army submit so very quickly?

Let me share some of AC's thoughts with you:[75]

"It hurts to lose. It hurts so much, you might even think I'm gloating. No. It is tragic the way the French memory works. He knows every inch of soil that was claimed by English Kings. He forgets about the war graves of the English soldiers who died to help France. There are so many streets and squares named for De Gaulle, Lattre de Tassigny, and others. But where can one find the tokens of gratitude to foreign heroes? Britain was the last country to stay free. All the others are soaked with forgotten British blood."

"The French mock the British for not having the 'European spirit.' This comes ill from farmers who burn British sheep alive. It is even worse when the government forms a joint army with the former enemy, Germany. Your victory cost Britain dear. She is still paying for it. But the old enemy has the strongest economy in Europe. Who would ever know that it lost the war?"

"Shame on you, France! You excuse the Second World War but stay indignant for ever about Agincourt, Calais and Waterloo. Vive la France! May you live long – long enough to see the tide turn. All those monuments to glory will not suffice to shelter the dying and homeless."

74. A special, friendly understanding established during the reign of Edward VII.
75. In some of these words, Aleister seems suspiciously prescient, as when he talks about the EEC, for instance. But many of these sayings have come via spirit seances, automatic writing and direct voice mediumship. Treat them as you wish.

I am sad to repeat such a message. Those are AC's own words and, remember, he worked for the French secret service. He should know what he's talking about.

Suspicions

The French citizen does not see how *frail* everything is, or how quickly it could all disappear.[76] Shakespeare said "All the world's a stage"[77] – well the scene in France has been bloodier than most. One has only to list the carnage – the massacre of the Cathars, the butchery of the Templars, the murder of the Huguenots, and the shameful Reign of Terror. Can't you see the dark forces at work? All of that was a stratagem. The aim has been: to stop France finding *her true power*.

France as she is known, is not the France that she was destined to be. The men who built Chartres cathedral were not seeking to let loose the violence in your breast. You have the highest level of fatal road accidents in the world. Crimes of violence done against children, women, old people and general society are rising. Rackets are rife. Paris is almost as bad as Naples for organised crime. You take more and more sedatives, there is more and more divorce, and more and more people are committing suicide. Even the spread of AIDS is quicker in France. *This* is not glory. This is not your *real* destiny.

Something else is at work – some other force which holds France back and sabotages her sources of true power. Of course, the plain Frenchman sees none of this. He doesn't notice how they turn his special genius into pure violence. But for how many years can they go on 'living in the past'? How long will they indulge their false sense of cohesion by mourning the death of famous people. "Five years already" the TV reminds them almost every week. At regular intervals, the media look back at dead artistes. This ever popular homage at the shrine of some *monstre sacrée* seems to provide a sense of unity. But if death can do this, why not true glory?

While Masonry designed the Revolution, it also helped many of the *ancien regime* to escape to England. Why? Well, you see,

76. "Sic transit gloria mundi": words spoken at the coronation of a pope when a tuft of wool is burned before his eyes. First recorded by Thomas à Kempis in the Middle Ages but probably much older still.
77. 'As You Like It' II, vii.

having wrested power from the autocrat, the last thing they wanted was for it be divided among the restless masses. The English had already tamed their own Kings. They'd had their revolution a hundred and fifty years previously. Quite wisely though, they had restored the monarchy and let the King live ... but with no real political power. In Britain, the Masons' aim is to protect the status quo, and keep control of things. They have been doing precisely the same thing in France ever since the days of the *Directoire*.[78]

78. An executive of five persons who ruled France (1795-9) just after the Revolution.

11
ALBIORIX

The Gallic god, Teutates, in his role as King of the World

The Law's Majesty

The Law has more than its fair share of Masons. Judges, lawyers, top police, the elected bodies, the armed forces ... at every level and in every arm, the canker is well embedded. As we all know, the law is not perfect. It does make mistakes; and it cannot always cover them up. Innocent men do get sent to jail. Innocent men have even been executed in the past. False evidence has been made up – by the police! The words of witnesses have been doctored – by the police! Suspects have been beaten until they confessed – by the police! What is hard for other citizens of Europe to realise is that a 'gendarme' is a member of the army. And the head of the army is ... ?

One must recognize that when Masons speak on their own behalf, they are not therefore telling the truth. And when they print pamphlets or make TV films ... one has to remember that mock American series: 'V' – for Vengeance. They control the facilities, they own the personnel, and if they don't pay the critics, then at least they hold power over the critics' own welfare. Believe me, I paused many times to wonder what stance my own publisher will take!

Have you noticed what happens when a member of the police commits a crime? In the last four years, they have robbed banks, stolen from shops, shot young victims, and even sold weapons to Iraq! Have you never noticed how long it takes for these cases to arrive in court? Have you not noticed how charges have been reduced along the way and how one or two persons have had the charges against them wholly dropped? The headlines only last a certain number of days. The camera turns its attention to more recent events.

God knows how often a case fades away simply because a vital piece of evidence has vanished. And everyone knows that if he rocks the boat – he can lose his job, he can get a visit from a Tax Inspector, or he can get his mortgage cancelled. Not to mention the fact that every gendarme who sees your car will inspect it for yet another fault. As the English proverb has it: "there are more ways of killing a cat than drowning it in cream."

They are brothers, you see. The links between them can stretch across frontiers. If you hurt one, you make enemies of them all – and almost all of them occupy quite important posts. Enough to make life hell, anyway, and enough to lose any dossiers it cares to. It wouldn't surprise me if they don't find the Bastille one day – that was probably stolen and not stormed.

The media are also involved. It doesn't matter what any of us do – buildings in Paris will be used as criminal holdings, and TV chains will die in front of our eyes. If I did not have some 'insurance', I would not have dared to publish this book in France. Luckily, I do not 'live' anywhere. I am always on the move, visiting groups in several countries, and I use several names. But despite all my caution, I have had some narrow escapes, as I told you in my earlier book.[79]

But the power of this country – the *real* power – rests in strange hands. Not even the CIA, the KGB, the British Secret Service or the Deuxième Bureau has ever been able to make contact. There are 'worms' at the core of all these apples. AC knew this, and he did get in touch. As I have said before, he also stole some very awkward papers as a kind of guarantee. Yes, I've got them now. They are lodged very carefully in non-legal hands.

It is quite on the cards that I might disappear, or meet a sudden and very strange end. If that should happen then, like my father, copies of those papers would be sent to every group of any influence in many countries. This would include the Stock Exchange, banks, Interpol and all the mass media. Without being too dramatic, I think there is a fair chance they might even destroy the EEC. So this is why they go on looking still. Half a century after AC's death, they are still jumping about like fleas on a griddle! Dear me!

79. 'The Riddles of Aleister Crowley'.

I have no intention to hurt anyone or damage any institution. But because they are not exactly in love with me, I derive a certain comfort from knowing that I make them nervous. Let them stay nervous – or let them own up.

Boxes in Boxes

Who are the Masons in the book industry?[80] It is no good jogging round the shops or printers to ask them. They are not likely to tell you. If they are Masons themselves, then they are under an oath of secrecy. Besides which, one Mason may be quite ignorant of any other person's links. That is why they have a weird handshake and secret signals. All good, clean fun, to be sure. I compute that about one third of the personnel are members of the Masons, and few have dawdled on the bottom degrees. I think that this piece of information helps one to explain their strange attitude to my books.

I have already quoted one literary expert, but it bears repeating: "It is an excellent read. Oddly, I doubt if anyone in England will publish it."

As with AC, so it is with me. That does seem rather to echo the words of Jesus Christ, but I'm not really as arrogant as all that. I realize, for instance, that AC wasn't God ... though he too did have problems with publishers. Or was it publicans?

There was a lot of fuss in the letter columns of 'The Times' to do with 'The Hess Affair'. I even called them from Hamburg. When I got through to the Letters Editor, he quite fairly told me to write a letter! Just to show that I wasn't a snob, I also called a few members of the gutter press. On each occasion things went fine until I mentioned the magic word 'Crowley'. That's when they advised me to ring again next April and slammed the 'phone down. These are the 'newshounds' who can smell a 'scoop' a mile away.

While all this was going on, I noticed a rather anguished letter for the MP for Edinburgh West, Lord James Douglas-Hamilton. This gentleman is the son of that same Duke of Hamilton, who was rumoured to have been behind Rudolf Hess' flight to Britain during World War II. The poor fellow was very keen to make the

---

80. See 'The Brotherhood' by Stephen Knight. Panther Books 1985, and its successor, 'Inside the Brotherhood' by Martin Short, Grafton Books, 1991.

government speak out, and clear his father's name. He did not get very far. Neither did he reply to my letter.

It rather seems that he passed it on to a colleague because I got a circular letter asking me for a free copy of my book. This came from a journal called 'Intelligence Quarterly', the editor of which explained that he had to 'keep' a database on matters to do with the secret services. Now, if he had lamented that he had "a wife and three starving children" to keep, I would have given him some succour. But he earns far more than I do, and so do the readers of his journal.

Well, if either of these MPs have read my second book, they will now realize that there were matters of grave concern involved. All British governments, since the Second World War, have understood *why* the Hess affair was best kept secret. So far as matters about the Royal Family were involved, nobody was going to risk stepping out of line! I don't think that this was due to some deep loyalty to the monarchy. It was a fear of the public unrest that might follow such misdeeds.[81]

Since the Communist Empire in Europe has now fallen, the KGB offices in Moscow have been put to pillage. Perhaps they will at last reveal something to confirm the stories I have told. But somehow, I doubt it. Russia now needs all the aid she can possibly get so I can't see her rocking any boats or upsetting any sources of charity. The Romanovs, let us not forget, had the blood of Queen Victoria in their veins! As for Masonry, it has not changed its values since the day it was first founded, a mere two or three hundred years ago! They all swore to protect the throne from any Catholic sway. But, of course, there is far more to it than that.[82]

By the way, chaps: it was a lovely 'Open Day'.[83] At last it is patently obvious to the entire world that those nasty stories which people say about you are totally unfounded. You put on a very good case to scotch all hostile rumours, and you most certainly assured me that you are really good chums to have around the place. But you are still very tricky enemies.

81. See Chapter 16, 'The Riddles of Aleister Crowley', Diamond Books, 1992.
82. Stephen Knight, ibid.
83. As a 'public relations' exercise, Freemasons' Hall in London was thrown open to the public in later summer, 1992. A friend of mine asked questions about Crowley's membership details. These had been 'misplaced'!

Russian Dolls

East Europe is in the same mess now as African colonies were when the colonial powers pulled out. One can only surmise about the cause. After the Second World War, you recall, England, France, Belgium and other colonial powers began to grant autonomy to their former domains. There was often a great deal of trouble. But in recent years, former French colonies have been tumbling, one at a time, into anarchy or civil war. Chad, Togo, the Ivory Coast, New Caledonia, Haiti and so on.

What can be the cause? Is the French language itself to blame? It is, after all, the only language which has an Academy whose duties include 'coining' new terms to keep up with the times. Not that I am in the least bit hurt by their semantic neurosis. I find it utterly charming. But French was once the international language for diplomacy. America and Russia changed all that. So now, the question of national influence is involved. Everyone in France deplores the growing intrusion of English. If it were German – perhaps they wouldn't be quite so upset?

One blatant result of this 'fear of English' has been that, alone among the nations of the world, France has invented its own words for computers. This has not helped at all in the realm of economic contest – nor in the matter of European team-work. Japan, Korea and Taiwan can export computers like hot cakes. But the French company, Bull, has had some set-backs. I can foresee the day when they will bitterly regret the agreement that has been made with the American company. Due credit must be paid to Mdme Edith Cresson, who was the prime minister.

"Most languages," AC said, "grow, develop and move ahead. The slang one spoke only yesterday, so soon becomes the accepted speech for tomorrow. French, however, has been embalmed in a dainty pose and stuffed like a three hundred year old goose."

"They flaunt it," he went on. "They are even proud of it. When they butchered their noble families like so many sausages, they no doubt spoke the death sentence in stylish grammar. Then, as if they rued all terror and excess, they decided to keep the language as a sort of souvenir. 'Look,' they seem to be saying. 'We are not savages after all.' "

"But a people are not the language that they speak! Perhaps someone should tell them," he said with a smile, "that pride is supposed to have led to the devil's downfall. But I'm sure they will reply that French is spoken by God." He wet his lips wickedly. "But not when He has the choice! And even then, he lets a Seraph interpret for Him!"

These are matters that concern France and the French. But it seems hard for them to realize that they are Europeans for whom the British have the greatest affection and warmth. When you, France, so European in outlook, order your radio and TV to play more French rock music – please try to understand why the rest of us find it funny. Our mouth corners twitch but not with malice or sneers. People who learn French are always taken aback by the lack of 'metre' and 'stress' in your speech. Much the same applies to Chinese. In China, the government is outraged when its youth dares to prefer Western music to the wilder moments of the Peking Opera. As you might expect, the French government does not like Madonna or Michael Jackson being quite so popular. Oddly enough, she suspects it is all a plot hatched by '*La Perfide Albion*'.

Well, they are correct about the plot, but they are wrong to imagine that Albion is behind it. Unlike the same Mdme Edith Cresson, most English people try to be polite and avoid causing hurt to other folk's feelings. We even try not to point out that the French language lacks all tempo and rhythm. Certainly, patriotic words can be imposed on it, along with the steady tread of a military march. It can also be sung rapidly, with extra vowels thrust in to make a flowery ballad. The music is fine. The poetry is fine. But they don't go together to make Rock and Roll.

Unless, of course, a young musician breaks the rules and resorts to 'Franglais'. If he does that though, he might lose all aid from the Ministry of Culture.

Message for Our Time
I'm in the mood for oracles. I hope you don't mind. I prefer them fresh, myself. They are so much more succulent, don't you think? It's no use my trying to stop them anyway. If they want to come, then they'll come. I might just as well help them out.

Of course, putting it all in print does mean that I have stuck my neck out. It's no longer just a faint whisper that I can deny ever having said. Should it prove to be false, or inexact, then I am stuck. Too bad. I'll still go ahead.

Now I'm not going to give you the vague waffle that one gets from starry oracles in the tabloid press. I will not talk about trends, possibilities, or latent forces. I'm not going to hedge my bets with a weather bulletin that forecasts both grey skies and blue, or sunshine and snow. I stick my neck out. Since I still have my head on, you may assume that I'm usually right.

1. Great Britain has a great deal to fear from its current political system. One more rider has joined The Four Horsemen of the Apocalypse. His steed streams with blood and has lost one eye. His name is Anarchy. When he comes he will bring the total collapse of the system. The angry rabble who follow him vapidly will be murdered in their thousands. None of them will live to regret what he has done.
2. France will need to plan a new Republic. But statesmen will be so afraid of anyone gaining advantage that the next republic will be as corrupt as the last one. I see civil strife again as the country marches on the city of Paris. Famous names will become joints of meat. The new nobility of films and TV will be torn to shreds by paupers' claws.
3. There will be bombs again in Germany and great men on whom the world pins its hopes shall fall. The shadows will rise and take on a new substance. But this time they will be victims as the Fatherland weeps like an old, old man.
4. The people of the Alps will be the most despised in Europe. It shall be shown how they became rich out of being 'neutral'. Despite their vast system of defence, they do not count on the whole of Europe attacking them. The Alps will fall, tunnels will close, and there will be famine in every Canton.
5. An army will rise against its own government and the rest of Europe will do nothing. This will cause grave problems for the EEC.
6. I see hordes of homeless – men with no jobs – mothers with no breasts and babies made of old twigs. I see the hungry marching on country estates and hunting blue blood in the Mayfair Mews.
7. I see ermine robes used as blankets. I see Hockneys being burned to take the chill off the air. I see famous faces in zoos and Ministers hanging by their feet from street lamps. Money will be useless. The FT index will be a term used by whores.

The legal system, from the youngest police cadet to the oldest Judge, will be fed to the ravening dogs.

8. The Prince of Darkness will be better prepared than the Prince of Wales. There will be glee but no jubilee. And when it is finished, it will all be over. Saint John was wrong. The trump will sound and then – eternal silence. No choirs in heaven nor any howls in hell. Not one shall remain. The Earth will waltz around the sun until, exhausted, plop!

9. No 'Who's Who' or 'Almanac Gotha'. No one to read. No one to give a shit. Just the sound blast of a last full-stop being stabbed in the Holy Book. And no National Anthem!

It's all a bit glum, isn't it? Well, it has to be, if people are going to take it seriously. If I were joyful you would not believe a word I said. In any case, you can if handle good news. It's the disasters you most want to hear about. This could be why we react so badly on learning that a baby is on its way.

12
ELAGABAL

The Syrian 'Lord of the Mountains'[84]

Great things are done when men and mountains meet;
This is not done by jostling in the street.[85]

Godly Mountains
In the Jewish faith, there are at least three sacred mountains, possibly four. The first is Mount Sinai, where Moses was given the Ten Commandments which he put in the Ark of the Covenant. The next is Mount Zion, the original Holy Hill on which stood the ancient city of Jerusalem. The third is Mount Tabor, near the Sea of Galilee. The fourth is Mount Ararat, where Noah's Ark grounded. Temple Mount has the remains of Solomon's house of God, but is also precious to Muslims who regard the Al-Akhsa mosque as the "farthest mosque" to which the Mahomet was borne during a night. They also value Mount Hira, where the Prophet prayed in a cave to receive the Word of God.

The idea of a Mountain being the home of Gods dates back almost to the beginning of time. In Ancient Greece the people stood in awe of Mount Olympus. In North Africa, they thought

---

84. Also known in Greek as Heliogabalus, or 'sun swallower'. The Roman Emperor, Julian the Apostate, revived the cult.
85. William Blake, MS Notebooks, p. 43.

the Atlas Mountains held up the sky. Sacred writings speak of mountains as being fired with Gods' power, and the site of divine visions. In contrast, valleys and plains are always shown as places of famine, pestilence and flood. The plain of Megiddo is destined to be the place of the battle which will end the world.

God is 'on high', and Evil is 'down below'. The virtuous tend to 'climb', while sinners always 'fall'. In many accounts of creation, the earth itself is quite smooth at first. But the war between good and evil thrusts up the mountains and lets the seas escape from the inner inferno. There is evidence of similar beliefs today, especially near to active volcanoes.

The people of Israel were cradled in ancient Egypt, where they were called 'Hyksos' or 'Shepherds'. They believed that the sun itself arose from a sacred mountain in the east and descended to another sacred mountain in the west. It was the purpose of a solar priest to ensure there was no obstacle to this daily voyage. In Great Britain it is visible in the monuments which may have been used in counting or as tools in astronomy. Stonehenge gives the news that the sun is at its zenith at the solstice.

The mountain is sacred not only because it is nearer the Gods, but also because it is farther away from the abode of men. It is a holy site, removed and at a distance. The mountain is therefore purer and nobler. What one does there will be more properly done for there will be less risk of sacramental pollution. There will be no taint from plain[86] things. There is no profanation.

The Navaho Indians believe that during the creation, Man and Woman called up seven sacred mountains. These are arranged in a special pattern: one at each point of the compass and three in the centre. There is a Persian myth which talks of the seven gods who live on a sacred Mountain. The Hindu tale of the 'World Mountain' which has seven sides, has had a profound effect in Aryan[87] culture. The link between the number seven and lofty heights echoes a belief that both are linked to the sanctity of life.

The Knights Templar were set up to defend pilgrims on their journey to the Holy Land. The Order built strong citadels, often on mountains, and the number seven or its symbol, featured prominently in them.

---

86. Plain = ordinary = or matters to do with the flat plains.
87. This is just another term for the Indo-European cultures.

Mystic Land

The notion of a Land amid the mountains is a very potent image. Tibet, for example, became a perfect spot on to which myths and legends could be projected. Being unlike European culture, it also had the helpful ingredient of being 'exotic'. Alexandra David-Neel was the first to explore the land,[88] as far as we know. She is even quoted by a member of the Tibetan Order of Kargyupta.[89] But another lady, Helena Blavatsky went further still by visiting the under-ground railway system, while Dion Fortune 'painted' the walls. One might well say that 'magical Tibet' was born of these three ladies.

Small wonder that fiction writers jumped on the same band wagon. 'Lost Horizon', by James Hilton, shows a paradise on earth. It is called Shangri-La, and nobody who lives there ever grows old. It made a hugely successful film and led to new types of cosmetics.

Atlantis was a myth made in Ancient Greece. No other evidence has ever been found, but that too gave new impulse to a type of occultism which would have done better to have used the creams of Shangri-la. In like vein, Madame Blavatsky spoke of the lost 'Land of Mu'. Since this did not exist, she met her 'secret masters' not in Lemuria, but in Tibet. Top notch persons, clearly. They used no socks or thermal underwear, yet they could sit in the snow and melt it in a six-foot circle round them. Quite why they would do this was never explained. But there is a brand of porridge oats that has the same effect. We have all seen the one but not the other.

Secret Masters had been known before, but not in quite that context. One thinks of people after the mould of Christian Rosenkreutz, The Count of St Germain or, closer to our own time, Fulcanelli. Until this, Masters were seen as gifted *human beings* who guarded the secrets of truth. Their name or identity was not the issue. What mattered was their knowledge.

This causes confusion among occult students. Many of them now believe that Masters do not reveal their presence, they have blue extremities, and they are entities half-way between Bodhisattva and a Traffic Warden. The editors of 'Chaos

---

88. cf. her books 'Tibetan Journey', 1932, and 'With Mystics and Magicians in Tibet', 1937.
89. Lama Anagarika Govinda, 'Foundations of Tibetan Mysticism', Rider, 1959.

International' think I am a fag-end from a blocked urinal. They should know! Still, you can see how absurd it is when occultists at the end of the twentieth century have their brains knotted by ideas from the nineteenth century. O brave new world, that hath such people in it!

My status does not matter. The truth is not altered one iota by the opinion of a million experts. The main thing about being a Master is that someone gave you the job! I wasn't too keen at the start. I turned it down for quite a few years. But now that I have taken it on, it really doesn't matter what anyone thinks. I can only teach those who wish to be taught. Of course, I can't say if the Gods are offended or not. That's your own affair.

How odd that God would plonk Masters in the middle of Tibet, exactly where they're not needed. And so out of touch, too! But Madame Blavatsky preferred it that way. "They know how to contact me," she declared. Right! Yes! I get it. If Aleister's one-time boss, Samuel Liddell Mathers, can be believed, they sometimes do it in the Bois de Boulogne in Paris. I should tell you that this is famous as the biggest open-air brothel in the world. Things like this can have a great impact if you are at an impressionable age. It boosted Mathers' self-esteem enough to make himself head of 'The Hermetic Order of the Golden Dawn'.

By the way, I don't want to throw the cat among the pigeons, but has nobody noticed the similarity between 'Ra-Hoor-Khuit' and 'Koot Humi'?[90]

Reputed Perfidy

When Colin Wilson[91] first raises the subject of AC's attempted ascent of Chago-Ri in 1902, he says of Crowley that "mountain climbing still continued to obsess him". Crowley was a student at the time! Later, he says that Crowley had a fever due to malaria. Nevertheless, when Crowley shot a duck, this revealed "the manic stamina that made him such a bad enemy". If ever Wilson has malaria, he will find that raving does occur. The famous Israel Regardie write that AC was schizoid. Wilson corrects him and uses the word "psycho". This is not a proper term but the title of a film.

90. The latter is a secret master, as reported by Mdme Blavatsky; the former is an image of Horus that was held dear by AC.
91. 'Aleister Crowley – The Nature of the Beast', 1987, Aquarian Press.

In his own account, Crowley takes fifty pages to describe the 1902 attempt to climb to Chogo-Ri. Today we call it K2. Wilson says that Crowley looked on it as more than a mere challenge to his skills. Well wouldn't you? It was the second highest mountain in the world. Wilson says it was an attempt to rectify some sort of flaw in Crowley's identity. While not shy of showing his lack of knowledge,[92] one begins to worry about Wilson's motive. When Sir Edmund Hilary was asked why he had gone up Mount Everest, he replied "Because it was there!" How does Mr Wilson diagnose that?

Madame Blavatsky had issued 'Isis Unveiled' in 1877, when AC was two years old. One can actually trace a connection between this book, via other people, to the founding of 'The Hermetic Order of the Golden Dawn'. Crowley did not join until 1898, when he was a ripe twenty-three. Young men still had dreams in those days. Today they take drugs. But the Book of the Law was dictated in a Cairo hotel in 1904 – only six years later.

What ambition! At the age of twenty nine, Crowley was trying to out-do Mdme Blavatsky! This was two years after the attempt to climb Chogo-Ri. Wilson remarks that, in terms of going up mountains, this was Crowley's first defeat. It was also, he adds, the prelude to the end of Aleister's life. Come, come, Mr Wilson! With forty more years still to go?

It is said that Crowley had a fierce dispute with another mountaineer called Jacot Guillarmod. Guillarmod went specially to visit Crowley in Scotland to persuade him to join the team. Crowley agreed, but only if he were the leader. John Symonds says that AC was so casual about Kachenjunga, he was almost blind to the risks. But Crowley was a top-class expert. Symonds is not.

We then get a series of petty hints and suppositions. Crowley had not provided the porters with footwear. I suppose not. Most people in Nepal wear their own. Guillarmod did not like the steps that Crowley cut in the ice. I don't suppose he liked his nose much either. When part of the team opted to leave, Crowley warned them of danger. One of them was killed in an avalanche. One man says he heard their shouts for help. Crowley did not. Wilson imagines that AC cackled and said, "Serves them right".

92. What a gripping task it might be to analyse Mr Wilson by examining the books he chooses to write and his personal use of language.

Symonds says Crowley went down the mountain and passed by the party as if he hadn't seen them. This was not St James's Park or The Strand. The winds at those altitudes make one deaf and snow glare reduces visibility to a few yards. Opinion is not proof. It suggests bile and envy. Even hate does not justify the use of weasel words. When a lawyer pleads "There can be no doubt" or "No one can deny", the more certain you may be that he is wrong. Why should John Symonds (who was not there) be more reliable than Crowley (who was there)? As for Colin Wilson, had he but looked at the source material, he would have noticed that Crowley's interest in mountains was as mystical as that of Gurdjieff.

Naturally, in this, as in all other things, each person will choose for himself what to believe. I am all for Crowley – which is not too odd, since I am his son. Messrs Wilson and Symonds are against him – which is very odd, since they have no obvious reason. Mr Wilson draws a line across the page. He thinks that the weight of evidence 'seems' to show that Symonds' account is nearer the truth. I ask again: what evidence?

Secret Masters

The opening words of the Latin Mass are: "*Introibo ad altare Dei*"... "I will go unto the High Place of God". That word 'altar' is how Greek scholars gave the Aramaic word for 'high place'. Only later did it come to signify a 'table'.

When AC made his mind up to invoke the demon, Choronzon, he enacted the ritual in Morocco. Along with Viktor Neuberg, he set out from the hamlet of Bou-Saada to climb Mount Dal'leh Addin. The date was the 3rd of December, 1909, which renders the number seven. In his account of his life, Crowley says that when the ritual failed, he hit on the bright idea of making a sacrifice of himself. For some reason best known to himself, Wilson deduces that this can only signify an act of buggery between the two men. Well, whatever it was that they did, they didn't do it for pleasure, eh? Indeed, after a little more sketching in of details, Wilson admits that something out of the ordinary must have taken place. Yes, indeed. *Crowley crossed over into the 'other' world.*

What befell him there led Crowley to the amazing insight that magic and sex were neatly bound. Either of them, or both, offer the means of crossing over. It was this wisdom which darkened Crowley's name as a dirty old man. Even worse, he was also a dirty young one. I got over the 'novelty' of being AC's son the same year that I found out. After that, I had to adjust to magic and learn how to use it properly. I found him cheerful. He made it easier to talk to him.

But in this age of science and vanity, it is hard being a man apart. I see light where others see shadows, and see shadows where they see only light. They treat me like a vagrant, so how may I speak without bias? Beside which, a man my age is not expected to whistle or sing. I have to be careful because I have enemies. I seem to have made them principally by not showing enough respect. I would not be the first prophet to be called mad. I would not be the only messenger to be stoned out of the town. But I am supposed not to criticize in case I make them angry.

I am angry. And with good cause. They have no excuse. Shall anyone blame me if I do what AC would have done? If I am truly his son and not, as they suggest, an impostor on the make – then wouldn't it be typical if I turned round and struck? "You should have proved it," they sneer. I will. They mean documents, of course. They want a piece of paper, signed by AC and witnessed by others. They want to hear someone was there at the time. Will my mother do? Or will it suit your purpose more to say that she is senile?

It doesn't even matter what evidence I might produce. They have decided beforehand not to believe it. They don't want to believe it. To believe it would demand too great a change in their view of the world. Their certainties would crumble. They could not be the same people that they are today.

I have got to be guilty. Any other verdict is unthinkable. And since it is unthinkable, it is also impossible.

No. Not really. I do have all the proof that your heart, mind and soul could ever desire. Forget the documents, the photographs, and the signatures. Think instead of 'The Occult'. If I am who I say I am then I ought to be able to do.

Read on, MacDuff!

13

THOKK

A Giantess who refused to weep for Baldur. One who is sworn totally to 'the Law of the Gods'

Hungers

There has been such a lot of rubbish spoken about these beings called Masters. First of all, there were Masonry's own secret chiefs. Then there was the kind of entities that arose from the dreams of Madame Blavatsky. After that, there were the things said by Dion Fortune. But when all this is put together, the scene was painted without one lick of truth. The idea would not have taken root so quickly unless it had touched a nerve! In addition, of course, most of these 'spiritual founders' rather fancied their Masters staying put, far beyond the reach of Tom, Dick and Harry.

For behold! It is quite true that 'Common Man' yearns for a source of magical authority. He has need of his unerring Pope, his Dalai Lama, his hallowed Emperor, or his 'Sacred King'. In itself, there is more than enough mystery to keep us awake at night. So during the 'romantic period', why on earth did they include yet more veils to obscure the mind?

Ours is a weary old world that we find humdrum, grey and tedious. Of course, I am talking about the developed world or what we often call the Western world. Elsewhere there are babies that look like rattles and old men that look like parched reeds. I don't mean them. We can forget about them. They have nothing at all to do with our right to believe what we want. They don't have that luxury. But we do.

I could mention the shady corners in London, Paris, Berlin or any other great city in Europe or America. I could show you the homeless, all cloaked like night commandos, who exist on the heat that seeps out of kitchens. They're like beetles and though we know they're there, we manage not to perceive them. We do not see them. We don't want to see them. Too many hands held out. They make us angry. Too many thorns that blemish our oh, so tender flesh. We would like them to go away please.

They're clumped close to the truth, you see, and we've got tickets for a West End show that will, hopefully, make us euphoric and forgetful. In a sense, this makes singers, dancers and actors just as criminal as the ones who sell drugs. They who entertain are in the same line of business as the arenas of Rome. Life is not a cabaret, old chums – it's a bloody circus. Yet still better than the coughs and sighs of the gutters.

So there are frenzied hordes of people hustling their souls for colour, jollity or events they can call 'an experience'. Play the music loud so their auditory nerves are numbed. Make the lights bright so their optic nerves are blinded. Give them a wall to bang their heads against – and while they are stunned, feed them your chemical truth. This is why they strut with energy, who are still powerless. This is why they walk on water, who believe they are workers of miracles.

This is why 'secret orders' and 'occult societies' sprout like fungus in a derelict house. They eat away at your substance and, in return, they provide you with some nice illusions. Dreams you can die to. Is it truly so arrogant when I declare that their opinions do not count as much as mine? Show me what good they've done that I may pay them reverence. Won't they please let us see how much progress they have achieved by their plans to save humanity? Apart from their officers, and councils, and cabinets – is there anyone at all whose life has been finer because of their existence? Oh please, tell them not to blush. Do not let them be quite so coy. Let them explain it to us just once: in what ways have they been unselfish?

Masters Again
Before I became a Master – before I became an Initiate even – I studied occultism at AC's knee. Once, when I was about twelve years old, he coached me in 'automatic writing'. When I produced something 'good' he would slip it into a folder and keep it safe. There was one occasion in particular when he was all but

stricken dumb by what I had written. He did some work on it himself – adding, cutting and changing – until it was almost a little book fit for publication. In view of what I have just been talking about, I offer the following extract.

Oh no! I feel it now
A pang of fear in my heart
As if a glove were splitting.
It wasn't just a swindle, was it?
Oh dear God, let the answer be no!
The heaven you showed me –
it wasn't just a sham?
I could not bear that.
I could not live with that.

Grand Orders with grades and degrees.
Beardless Masters with ankles on knees
I kissed your feet, didn't I?
I burnt incense to your holy, halo ego.
We were a thousand miles from Jerusalem
On the ferry that crossed the Styx.
It was a soft summer evening
and we watched the drowned drift by.
You pointed at the sunrise and said
Follow the sweet bags and tears.

Oh, why did you pilfer all my hope
When I was only out there begging?
I thought I was a High King
On a burning boat to Valhalla.
In the middle of a sandstorm
where a Dervish whirled.
And I did contemplate my navel
on platform number seven
Where the red rails had been rusting
Since the year the Prophet died
By suicide
To make atonement for
the fact that he had lied.

"Is this where I wait?"
I asked the strutting Guard.
"If this is where you wish," he said.
"The end is everywhere."
And then I saw the Truth that counts:
There are no pockets in shrouds
And we are not just of the same blood
But trodden from the same clay.
It was then that they came for me
And led me to the special seat
Where the whole world sat
In the maniacal dignity
Of the brotherhood beyond.

The Pilgrim's Last Prayer: 'Liber Fulgur', 1942
Aleister and Amado Crowley.[93]

I am a Master. So was AC before me. It is not a fitting title – it means so many different things these days. In former times it meant: 'One who has been given authority'. Quite simply that, and nothing more. You were lucky to find a Master willing to take you on. You were fortunate indeed to find one who would sign an indenture for seven years. It mattered not a damn whether he was Master Butcher, or Master Spinner – you sweated for your keep until he said you were qualified. There were no wages.

If we consider a Druid or an occult Master, the training could last for 'one third of your lifetime'.[94] If you remember the facts, AC told mankind that he was verified[95] as Master in 1915 – when he was forty years old. He was "delayed" he told me, "by the lack of a personal Master". AC felt that Eliphas Levi was his guide. But since the chap died the year of Aleister's birth, all contact between them was 'on the astral'.

Pie in the Sky
I must assert, in full gravity, that no student can suitably be informed by books or lessons that come by post and drop through

---

93. The origin of 'Liber Fulgur' is explained in my first book: 'The Secrets of Aleister Crowley', Chapter 14.
94. i.e. for twenty-one years.
95. He used to say that he was "condoned"!

a letter-box. Neither do I put very much faith in the kind of teaching that is provided at weekly meetings 'of a group'. Yes, these methods are very helpful these days, but they are adequate only if rounded out by regular meetings with the real, live Master. Certainly, a Master could write a book as well as he can give a lecture. But it is not just a question of the words that he conveys. His presence may also transfer a touch of mystic power which alone is capable of acting as a magic catalyst.

Neither AC nor I – nor, come to that, any other genuine Master in the world – would ever suggest that it is the happiest of callings. To parody Noel Coward: "Don't let your sons be Magicians, Mrs Worthington!" Somewhat like the carnival career of your average actor, life has ups and downs – but on an awfully colossal scale, if you follow me. This is not one of your nine-to-five jobs like a clerk or a cook. You are not free to pick out your clients, like movie moguls or whores. You can't fix your own fees or display a list of prices. You are obliged to take them – rich or poor, thick or gifted, handsome or haggard – as they come. All that is needful is that they satisfy the terms of the occult law.[96]

As destiny will have it, my students are all poor, thick and haggard but, happily, I refuse to read anything into that.

Of course, I cannot speak for mystic orders or occult societies. I don't know how they select their members. I don't even know if there is any selection at all. To judge by their pamphlets and other literature, it does rather seem that anybody can get in. Everyone is eligible – so long as he can pay his fees and dues. What can I say, apart from the fact that I'm surprised? How little this resembles the bygone 'School of Magic' where one studied free and worked for the gods.

If I criticize them too heavily then it must seem that I should criticize AC too. But as I've pointed out, he was a Master. His ways were not the ways of ordinary men – and my ways are not necessarily the same as his. He gave me my training, yes. But he did not brand my forehead like a herdsman nor did he claim that I belonged to his school. He did not make me a Master, you see. Such an act did not lie within his gift. He got me ready to the best of his ability, but the Overworld gave me my function.

96. They must prove that they will be good students, and you must guarantee success.

I know all that AC knew – and more. But I speak as they tell me to. I do not market my magic, although I am entitled to live by it. I work for my bread, just as other persons work for theirs. They have their jobs. I have mine. Each of us has his own task and therefore we are equal. I give my best, they give theirs, and everyone shares the good of the harvest. If I succumb then they will perish with me. If they died without sons, I would die too. I help them with my magic. I counsel them with my wisdom. I instruct them in the ways of the Gods and, when necessary, I journey beyond in their service and aid. That is the Law. That is the way of things. I must not have more wealth than they. If I become affluent, for example, by writing books, then I am obliged to share it all with others until the balance is reached again.

Why should this be so? The answer is quite simple. I am a Master, you see, and I already possess far more than other men. If they are to accept me, they with their faults and failings, then it has to be made obvious that I have also made a sacrifice. If I lived better than they, inequity would blind them. If I hoarded all the various benefits which they value, then I should shame them in front of their own families. I am not allowed to do good for myself. I may not do magic for my personal gain. The gifts are there for the sake of others. With powers like mine, one lives and works for the sake of friends. If it is required of me, I must be prepared to die.

How it Happened

It sounds a bit poncy, doesn't it? It sounds like one of those ripe, red clerics as fat as Eunuchs and voices like toasted muffins with jam. Well, if the ideas impress you as a bit too pious or splashy, then it could be this which hampers your feeling for truth. You're not a child. It's high time you put away your toys. You've got to understand that it's one thing to 'play' at magic but another thing to be consumed by ecstasy. Put all your gadgets in a drawer. Strip off your badges and trinkets. Just for one moment in your young life, stop striving to express yourself. Stop beating your chest and screaming "Look at me! Oh look at me!"

Make your world go silent and Listen. Snuff out your candle and creep behind your eyelids. Spit on the incense and let your nose catch the aroma of dusk or dawn. Be one with nature and do nothing, nothing, unless it will enrich her beauty. Begin by seeing just how trivial you are – and then grow. Let every thought that finds space in your head be a spangle of gold. Let each of your emotions be as clear as the lustre of a diamond. Of your own being, build a basilica where the Gods may enthrone you as King.

I can speak with a certain tilt of assurance because, to be sure, I did follow that self-same path myself. Aleister started my teaching when I was seven years old, and he made me an Initiate when I was fourteen. But I did not become a Master until my late twenties. What took place in between? Why was the wait so long? You know my story by now. I left school and spent just a year in some audit offices. I did my National Service and then I went to University. Then I hustled as an assistant in one of those huge mental hospitals where a map is essential to avoid getting lost.

I was poorly paid. It stopped one from quitting if one hadn't the price of a taxi. Very few of the staff 'lived in'. The Institute had quarters, of course, which were as cheerless as monastic cells, and there was the nightly risk of being called to an emergency. The two sexes were mixed and they mingled rather more than was healthy. Most of the female nurses were Catholic girls. They hung rosaries on their doors to show when they were in. There wasn't one of them who hadn't offered her virginity several times in the hope of catching a young doctor.

It was roughly the same with male nurses, barring the fact they were staunchly gay and worked wonders with locks. Were they like that before taking up employment? Had they all been hit by the same type of job jeopardy? Or were they martyrs of a sort, resisting the popish plot of the ladies? There was I, with my degree in psychology, and there were they offering me the wisdom of their rich, personal experience. "You will know that you are cracking," they told me, "when you start leaving your door unlocked!" It was then that I learned 'Salve Regina' in Latin. It means "Hail, Holy Queen"![97]

The lads took it all in very good part, with much eye-lid batting and hints of intrigue. I got a bit worried when I found that one of them was Catholic too. They all began to reply

97. It was a favourite prayer that the Irish girls used to address to the Virgin Mary.

in Latin, "*Gaudeamus igitur, dum sumus iuvenes!*" This becomes, a little roughly: "Let's whoop it up while we're young enough!"[98]

That is why I started going for long walks whenever I could get away. That is how I met the spirits on the moors. At this distance in time it is difficult to say whether I was driven to meet my destiny by theology or deviance. Or perhaps it was even some subtle, alchemic fusion of the two?

---

98. It is also the first line of a sort of 'school hymn' sung by German students. It is referred to in 'The Academic Overture', by Brahms.

14

WODEN

The Master of Wode, or war paint, and God of Wrath

Wilderness
The Pennine moors in the North of England are like nowhere else in the world. There is heather and its smell. They undulate for miles, like an angry sea, crested with rocks, ferns, and boulders. You walk for hours then, unexpectedly, you come across a ribbon of road. Follow it and, sooner or later you'll find a timeless pub. It's like a scene from 'Wuthering Heights'. There is 'The Great Western', named for the road from Sheffield to Manchester. Another is 'The Floating Light', on the way from Marsden to Oldham. People come to take a stroll now. In my day, there were fewer cars.

I remember the colours – slate, dark green, and dirty purple. But what struck me the most was the utter solitude. There were a scantling of sheep, looking like tufted door-mats. There was also the occasional hawk. But mainly one was alone. I suppose that sailors are not unnerved by the vastness of the sea. Neither does the moor's immensity upset you, if you are looking for calm. If you're a child of the city, this amount of space can leave you gasping. You have to stand like a stone in case you panic. You hear the faint sighing as the wind combs the hills.

There are hardly any walls or fences. At the edge of a road, perhaps, a few strands of rusty wire. But almost everywhere you come across these tufts of raw wool, torn off sheep's backs as they shuffled round or under something. Grey, greasy tatters that you don't recognize at first. Is it fungus, you wonder? Is it some sort of strange weed? But nothing grows here except the heather and, by the isolated black pool, tufts of reeds.

Here and there, quite widely spread apart of course, there are enormous black lakes. In fact they are reservoirs, which supply drinking water for towns and cities a hundred miles around. Most of them were built during the last century. There are local tales of historic tragedies – at Holmfirth, for example, – when the dams burst and swept hundreds to their death in the lower valleys.

The weirdest thing, which gives you a weak feeling in your legs, is to see parts of a village half submerged. On a cloudless day, down in the malachite depths, you can see a church tower, or even a graveyard. We used to go there, me and my mates, to swim in the arctic water. Once we climbed in the boarded window of a big empty house. It was weird to walk among old furniture, all draped in sheets. They had meant to come back, but the sheets were rags.

There was a ball-room with flecked mirrors, and a parlour with a table and fifty chairs. The floors were marble. When we opened the doors to the cellars, it was only water, with bottles bobbing like flotsam round a sunken ship.

Elsewhere, a mill-owner from Meltham defied the moors and built a designer house. It was in magazines. When the wool trade fell, it was left to die. The trees wilted. The lawns were seared by wind. A pane of glass broke, then windows followed. In the night, the roof lifted and the landscape was littered with slates. The sheep did the rest – plus the snow, the rain and some children.

All that was left was a concrete replica of the statue called 'David'. It was the version without a discreet leaf. He stood there nude, rude and rampant. Sheep scratched against it.

"Still good for summat," said the locals.

During a severe frost, it split into several pieces.

"It's been in the wars," said the men.

"It's withered from under use," snapped the women.

Lady of the Moors

Permit me to offer a few, disparate facts. This might be a good moment to draw them together and spy out what truth they hide.

In the ancient tenets of the Christian church, the Virgin Mary spent her last years in Ephesus, whence she was eventually assumed into paradise. In AD 451, in the same city of Ephesus, Mary was declared to be 'The Mother of God'. This had been well planned.

Before Christ, Ephesus was home to 'The Black Ephesian', also known as Artemis. A statue in the National Museum of Naples, shows the goddess with black face, hands, feet and multiple breasts. She wears a tower as a crown. This is not the Greek Artemis who was widely known in Arcadia.[99] (*Et in Arcadia Ego*[100])

The Emperor, Severus (AD 222-235) is called the Arkite. He was born in the Temple of Alexander at Arka in Lebanon. He devised a religion where many great names were elevated to the status of Gods.[101] In the Book of Genesis (X,17), other Arkites are mentioned, along with reference to Nimrod (i.e., Orion) and people linked with the Queen of Sheba. These were devotees of Astarte, or Ishtar, the goddess to whom Acacia wood was sacred.

For the Jews, the Ark of the Lord was also made of Acacia wood. At first it signified the holy objects being carried within, but in time it became the chest itself. It was the symbol of *Shekinah*, or God's eternal presence among his people. Others say that the son of Solomon and Sheba took the Ark to Ethiopia.

The Joan of Arc,[102] was close friends with Gilles de Rais, later executed as a black magician and a murderer. She also knew René de Anjou, a one-time member of the so-called '*Prieuré de Sion*'. It is interesting that she should have acquired this handle to her name, i.e., 'Joan of Arc'. More frequently, in French and in English she is referred to as 'The Maid of Orleans', i.e., The Virgin.

The British leader, known as King Arthur, together with his knights of the round table, was called '*Arcturus*' in Latin, i.e., 'He of the Arc'. He pulled a sword out of an 'anvil' to prove he was king. But it wasn't an anvil. It was a black stone, called 'The Arc'.

Moses, the man whose magic was greater than that of Egypt, was given the tablets of black stone by God, on Mount Sinaï. He broke them in fury when he saw the people adoring "the calf of gold".

99. A mountainous district in the Peleponnese which came to be seen as the ideal type of rustic paradise.
100. I am making a reference here to the symbolism used not only by Freemasons but also by the painter, Poussin. The title of one of his more enigmatic works is 'Et in arcadia ego' which can also be translated 'and I in the safety of the Ark'.
101. e.g., Abraham, Jesus, Orpheus and Alexander the Great.
102. Note the title, not unlike the Virgin of Orléans.

There is a black stone in the Ka'aba in Mecca. This is said to be a meteorite and to have fallen from the sky like 'a messenger from God'.

In France there is the greatest assembly of 'Black Virgins' in the whole world.[103] One hundred and ninety of them were recorded in the mid-sixteenth century. The greater number lie in a triangle formed by Vichy, Aurillac and Le Puy.[104] When one of them is destroyed by war or fire, it is replaced as soon as possible. The most famous is in Chartres cathedral, at a spot that was once the centre of druidism in Europe.

The church says that none of these statues is black by design. They have all turned black, she claims, as a result of incense, fire, or ancient efforts to lay on gold-leaf. Their names suggest otherwise. Many are known locally as La Mère Noire, La Nègre, La Brune or even 'Saint Mary the Egyptian'.

They are abiding traces of an ancient cult of the Earth Mother. Their vast quantity in France shows that churches were built on sacred sites where these statues were found. Some scholars say she depicts 'The Queen of Sheba', others 'The Mother of Harlots' and a few 'The Whore of Babylon'. In a sense she's the female element, the fertile earth, and the realm of shadows under the ground.

The Harlot Axiom

In the moors, there is another Black Stone. It is situated on Black Hill, on a part known as 'Saddleworth Moor'. It lies close to where the boundaries meet, which once divided the three parts of the ancient Danelaw.[105] It has been there longer still. The local stone is called 'millstone grit'. This is more like a meteorite.

Examine the chart[106] of my earlier book, and you'll see that Black Hill is close to a sub-group, at Oldham, and another at Buxton. Another thing: the locals don't talk about it. They will deny that any such stone is out there. They say it doesn't exist.

103. Ean Begg, 'Cult of the Black Virgin', Arkana, 1985.
104. S. Saillens, 'Nos Vierges Noires: leurs origines', Paris, 1945.
105. That part of N. and N.E. England which was occupied by the Danes in the 9th and 10th centuries. These lines now divide the three counties of West Yorkshire, Lancashire and Derbyshire.
106. On page 184, 'The Riddles of Aleister Crowley', which lists the structure of Crowley's New Order called: The Lamp of Invisible Light.

And yet – it is visited. Purely by chance, of course, while the Hippies are ruining Stonehenge, many people dawdle there on Midsummer's Eve.

What does he say, a man who is boozy and depressed? "My wife doesn't understand me!" What do the girls say after being arrested at midnight? "You don't understand, Your Honour. I was looking for a light and he cricked his back."

Well, I do not drink and I'm not depressed, and yet I'm not well accepted by the 'occult brethren' of this world. Needless to say, a lot depends on what you mean by brethren. I have a sad file of letters from souls who are mentally ill. I have another file, of letters from societies, orders and clubs. I have one or two from Envoys of God. Perhaps I should publish them. You could then decided who is more deluded.

Many an odd-bod calls himself an occultist. Often, he lives a secluded life, in a cold flat, and does an occasional 'banishing ritual'. His main need is for spiritual strength. He feels so weak in face of the system – but without that system, he would die of hunger. He is angry, not grateful. He is ashamed that he has to take such help. So he's ready to ruin society. He is willing to join with others and form a sort of social blood-clot. He is told that this is anarchy. But no. It's a form of suicide.

They form their own orders sometimes. They do not realize how deeply they are in the labyrinth of black magic. I am sorry for them. That will offend them. They don't want pity, even though they need it. What they want is Anger, Fury or anything else that has an effect. They want to count. Life is so boring, they value nothing and least of all – themselves.

Just think! If they had been Adam and Eve, there would have been no human race. But are they – or their puppet masters – still aiming for the same result? I've got news for you, lads. Defiance is not bravery! Intelligence means not blowing up the bridge that you are standing on. The awful, hollow misery is – you will never know why you failed. But ... if it keeps them off the streets ...

Imagine all the trollops of the world being herded into Hyde Park. As is their wont, Christians would try to burn them. The Socialist would try to liberate the ones at the bottom. The 'Greens' would try to protect the clover. The anti-hunt lobby might hack the fur-wraps off their shoulders.

The Old Testament[107] says a lot about sacred harlots. The males are *Kedeshim*, and the females *Kedeshoth*. Other faiths had them too. There were many in Greece and Rome. Mary Magdalen was one, if memory serves me right. They existed in an unstable society, where marriage and family were under threat. Prosperity needs laws of heritage, and men want to know their own sons. So sex became 'improper'. This means it was banned for common folk. This was not the case among the clergy, the aristocracy and the rulers.

In ancient Greece, the figure of Oedipus stood for ultimate sinner ... and also a sacred being. Having done so much evil, he was on a different level of being. That's still how it is with an 'outcast'. Not only were whores pushed to the edge of society, but masters and shamans too. The figure of Mary Magdalen, the reformed wanton, is often painted.

The High Place

I was alone. I swear to you that I was alone. I ambled at a very lazy pace, sometimes looking at the hummocks of heather around me, and sometimes raising my head and scanning the horizon. There are so few landmarks that you cannot always tell where you are. A local man might have a name for each hill and be able instantly to say which was which. He would have walked all over them. I was only a visitor.

All of a sudden, as sharp as a clap of thunder, the atmosphere changed. It was like the sensation I had when I was still a schoolboy[108] – of some invisible entity bearing down on me, like a huge hand.

I looked around nervously – well, no, nervously is not quite the right word for it. I was fearful – by which I mean I knew that I was no longer alone. The hairs on my wrist tingled. I swear to you, there was a fine line of light around my body, as if I were a cloud with a silver lining.

I knew that I was not alone, but I daren't look up for quite some time. It was like that magical moment when the groom is silently screaming for the bride to say "Yes". It always feels so much longer than it actually is. Isn't it strange how one's

107. Deuteronomy 23,17
108. Described in 'The Secrets of Aleister Crowley', Chapter 22: 'The Sand Pit'.

emotions can have this effect? I felt paralysed by a sense of holy terror.

When I did manage to look around, there were seven figures, each about half a mile away. They were so far from the horizon that intelligence knew they could not have walked or run. They had appeared, just like that. They came toward me as if they were floating. They stopped a hundred yards off and each raised an arm. It reminded me of a butler asking you to wait in the library, please. Not that I'd ever met a butler, but I'd seen them in films. But whereas they had always been dressed in smart suits, these persons were draped in greyish green robes, the colour of lichen on old stones.

They gestured toward the nearby hill and as I walked toward it, I too felt that I must be gliding. It never entered my head to be worried. If I'd had the sense, it might have flashed through my mind that these were robbers. But no, the terror within me was not a fear for safety. Somehow or other, I knew what they were, and I was utterly safe.

We stood before a small cave. In pelting rain, it would have sheltered four grown-up men, squeezed up tight. We were some three yards from it, but as we moved, the distance got longer and the cave higher. By the time we entered, I was boy-size again, and all around was a cathedral. If we had shrunk, I reasoned, then grains of sand should now be man-sized boulders. But they were still sand. This was no illusion. It wasn't a trick from a film. We had simply passed through a door. We stood in the Other World where things are different.

I'd like to share all that happened, but no words exist. There is no secret, but the barrier is your mind. AC took this step at the age of forty. It happened to me at twenty-eight. I was able to think in new ways. That is the difference between losing one's reason and being led by unreason. One goes beyond the point where it is relevant. "In the land of the deaf," asked Aleister, "who could you talk to? In the land of fools, we must teach."[109]

When I left the cave, I was still a man ... but a man who had seen the Gods. I was awed and appalled by the size of the task. A man wants to be like his own kind. But they made me a being apart. No, not better, not worse, but lonely.

109. Michael Apostolius, 'Proverbs', 15th c. "In the country of the blind, the one-eyed man is king."

15
NANNA

Lord of Destiny, and the Moon-God of Ur, in Sumeria

The Clan

AC wrote a certain number of books. He also wrote a quantity of articles, papers, poems and letters. The catalogue contains only those things which have been published at some time or another. Unless AC has had far more luck than George Bernard Shaw, or most other writers, there must be a lot of material that never did get into print. This fact is tempting for someone with a typewriter at the pawnshop, so let us all be careful about what we buy!

Now a lot of Crowley's work was of doubtful merit. This is one point on which Gerald Yorke and I agreed. In fact, we came to the conclusion that 'most' of AC's books were produced for money, and very little else. Now if anyone knew about these things, it was Gerald Yorke. He, and Karl Germer, were always willing to help AC, and in gratitude he let them 'take care' of his accounts. AC was not a literary giant. What he wrote has very little serious worth. Opinions at the time were dead against him. Unlike today, critics could then write English.

But, like hula-hoops, his stuff has a certain rhythmic popularity. Or to put it another way: it has a great commercial value. This does not mean that I feel that AC wasted his life. His real thoughts, his genuine discoveries, and his own vision of truth – these were not written down. They were transmitted face-to-face with just a few chosen individuals. Yes, I was one such person. I do not think I was alone.

But because of the 'money' aspect, I am pretty sure that a few 'unknown volumes' will rise to the surface from time to time – most probably when the original copyright runs out, in four years time. Many people will have recognized the golden opportunity and may already have begun putting pen to paper. There will be a sudden surge of fairly insipid texts. Why wait until copyright has run out? Is that what puzzles you? That's simple. Then, and only then, can we be totally sure that executors and heirs won't get their hands on it.

Now so far as I am aware, I am the youngest and the last of Crowley's own children. I must confess that, on this point, one can never be sure. He was a bit careless where he left things, and even as he grew older, he remained quite vigourous. Ginseng wasn't in it. All the same, I have children. So do my 'brothers and sisters'. I have checked up on as many of them as I could, and I've counted heads. We make up quite a nice clan – or battalion.

I have counted seventeen children, sixty-four grand-children, and one hundred and three of great-grand-children. This adds up to a total of one hundred and eighty-four people. Not all of them want any fuss, which is understandable. The members of most occult orders prefer to hide themselves coyly behind an occult alias. Even so, this is quite a sizeable bunch of 'Crowleys'. It would look extremely odd if any occult group chose to take us on. How would they explain that they were genuine adepts of AC – while suing or silencing each of his descendants?

The Anti-Clan

There are two groups of self-declared admirers and friends of AC who, I hope, will read my message. This will be difficult because, like the Freemasons, they have all been ordered not to read my books but use them instead as dart-boards. I am in both senses very holey.

I hear that you are anxious to get your hands on anything and everything that ever belonged to AC. Does that include the dried turds I found in Sicily? They would go wonderfully with Kenneth Anger's collection of doors. And if you really do want everything, does that include me? Please sirs, are you going to be my new daddies? I am not quite sure if I would care to sit on your knees – however many of them you've got!

There is one point that might interest the general public – and even the fair-minded members of these occult orders. What is the total amount of money that Crowley's books have brought in to date? Not one member of the family knows. None of the one hundred and eighty-four people with a blood-line has ever heard. Neither has anyone else. But imagine – please do it just to satisfy my whimsy – imagine that a 'Last Will and Testament' came to light. Yes, yes, you'd do everything in your power to prove it was a fake, and so on. But just suppose that in spite of your efforts to defend your own interests, such a document did exist. It might. It just might. Then what would be the total sum you might owe to the legal heirs ... with compound interest added?

No. I have to point out that I am not uttering any threat at all. As a matter of fact, if someone says he might decide to go to law – the law does not think 'it' is ever a threat. Never, never believe that you can 'threaten' or 'menace' people with justice. On the contrary: when someone tries to stop you going to justice – when someone tells you that if you do, even worse things will be revealed – that is blackmail, aggravated by menaces, and it is a crime. I have already been 'advised' by anonymous letters and by telephone, that my health would certainly suffer if I caused any more waves. I am very deeply shocked, as must you be, to learn that there exists a sort of 'Occult Mafia'.

But it seems to me that everyone is forgetting one thing. I can understand that anyone might suspect that I am not AC's son. I suppose that such a possibility is appalling and represents such a disaster to their own affairs – that they could just bring themselves to dismiss all evidence, even all proof. They don't want me to be Amado Crowley. But isn't this made obvious by the fact that they resort only to ridicule?

I can see why they would not want to sue me. The publicity might be bad for them. Beside which, there is a doubt, and the judge might accept my case. But they would also have to prove that I gained some advantage from making such a claim – and I would have to show what advantages they stood to lose.

So, since they are occult orders – why don't they use magic? Why don't they shut me up by sending demons, seven plagues, or mental illness? It costs far less than an English solicitor. It is very easy to do ... if you possess the necessary authority. Now, just pause and ponder this point – if they have the slightest doubt about me – they know that AC would be on my side and that I would possess more power than ever they could imagine.

With becoming modesty, I have to say that I am not just a pretty face. Many would say I'm not even a pretty face, but that's beside the point. I have been placid, non-hostile and content just to be left alone. But you have provoked me too much. I have borne all that I'm going to bear. There is a point at which even a White Magician is allowed to fight back. I have already started on a postcard of a donkey. A little further on, I will widen the scope. May the spittle dry in the mouths of those who spit.

Witnesses

In this, my third book, I am happy to report that my account of Crowley's life is gathering more and more evidence. If ever a show-down comes, there has been a dramatic shift in ground. And who can say but what Crowley's spirit may be out there – looking in at those who are looking out. To whom did Crowley bequeath all his magic powers? Or must we assume that these energies died with him? This is puzzling. More than that, it is a mystery that few men can penetrate. Whatever your age, you brain cannot imagine what 'death' may be like. It can only deal with events it has experienced. Now many people are frightened of death and dying *simply because* it lies outside their ability to cope.

It follows therefore that not even a religion, let alone an Occult Order, can be certain. If they 'knew', why would they go on in hymns, prayers and sermons, constantly telling themselves that they know? As Dr Goebbels[110] knew, repetition alone can be accepted as proof by the brain. So what do these Occult Orders think about what happened to AC after he died? And do they ever take seriously the fact that they cannot predict when they will join him?

People join these orders in the hope of achieving certain ends. But those who manage the orders, have not achieved these ends themselves. Do their sonorous and majestic titles mean that they are fully ready to go through that last door? It would be fascinating to find out. But I suppose, like the rest of us, they will just have to curb their eagerness and wait. Unless, of course, they get some inside information, as I do. But even there, I cannot accept that the Shade of AC would be telling *both* of us we were right.

Now one might anticipate, that where huge sums of money are concerned, even the most exalted institutions can lose their cool.

---

110. The chief of Hitler's propaganda service.

It is an episode to which the Church never refers, but its bank had financial connections with the Mafia and the P2 branch of Masonry. The Italian press named names, and the Mafia embassy to the Holy See began to talk. Now since scruples did not stop anyone then, why should they do so now? Let me put it another way: why would the authorities check the Vatican for electronic bugs? One does not have to be terribly shrewd to calculate two things: 1 – There are things it needs to keep secret; 2 – There are people who need to break the secrecy.

But, you might protest, this is a church! This is a body which takes care of things spiritual. Quite so! But there are matters it does not wish anyone to know about. Your own lack of curiosity does not alter the facts.

An ignorant person – one who does not and also one who dare not doubt – would assert that the Church does not meddle in politics. As myths go, that almost beats the one about Atlantis. What the Pope says about contraception has enormous impact on the social services and the economy of a country. He took advice from a group which met at the English College in Rome. He was told that this was the only way to be certain that a soaring birth rate would be mainly Catholic.[111] By hook or by crook, they mean to replace Communism with their own ideology.

Naturally, it does not enter their heads, but it is one thing to be born a Catholic – quite another to 'be' one. The birth-rate is falling in France, Spain, Italy and Ireland. It is even less in the Vatican. Are we to assume that only Catholics are being affected by the fall-out from Tchernobyl? Or do those who cheer the Pope quietly ignore his advice? In either case, it is a very bad sign. The church is losing its authority.

My data was not leaked by the Swiss Guard. It doesn't come from a silenced priest or disgraced bishop. I get it from someone in 'Opus Dei'[112] who is a convinced occultist. He says that the same situation applies in Occult Orders, Societies and clubs. The power is drying up. Like the 'The Phantom of the Opera', they let the mask slip and people have seen the other half of their sordid

111. For several thousands of years, the world population used to be stable at a few hundred thousands. It is now about five billion. It is expected to double again in the next eight years.

112. An extremely devout and right-wing 'fraternity' that originated in Spain and whose activities have often been questioned over recent years.

face. So, I repeat my question. Do they believe in Crowley's power? Do they think he approves of what they do? And when they cross the bridge, with what shall he welcome them?

Motive & Money

Are you bitter? Is contempt the best response you can come up with? Ignore me, by all means. But you do wrong to insult me. I am doing good things for AC. It is strange that you object. Fortunately, it is not an Occult Order which makes or un-makes Masters. After so long without one, you must be feeling the pinch. Looking at some of the folk you have promoted to high degrees, you must even be desperate. AC has been under constant attack, and none of you has lifted a finger. Yet when I stick my head out, you sneer even louder than his 'enemies'. Remember Goliath, my dear chaps.[113] Just think what Samson did with the Middle Pillar! I speak for AC. You speak for your own ambitions.

He was right to hide me. God knows what would have befallen me if he had put me in your care. He knew I'd be a thorn in your side. Maybe he even planned it. No doubt you think you deserve all you have got. I'll go further. I think you needed it. The fact that you grabbed it with all four paws fulfils a certain prophecy.

No one doubts that Crowley was a Master, not even those who attack him. So I draw some comfort from your attacks on me. You shall stand by your statements when you are called to account. You never gave me a hearing. Your verdict was made the same second you knew that I existed. Why were you so quick on the draw? Or, to put it another way, what makes you sensitive and scared?

An unbiased person must find your conduct curious. You behave like people who have cornered the market, and try to bully anyone who seems to be in competition. I beg your pardon. Silly me! I though we were all in the business of sharing the truth with others. But I would rather be naive than cunning. My simple spirit thought you would be glad that a bit of Crowley still lived. So did he, it seems. He gave me a message for you. It was very awkward for me when you never bothered to ask for it.

Perhaps you are testing me? Yes, yes, that must be it. You have been putting me through an ordeal for twenty years. You want to

113. cf. The Bible, I Samuel, 17.

106

be sure I've got his blood. You'd like to know if I've got his punch. Oh yes. I do know how to sock it to them.

Pipe-Dreams
By the way, I'm surprised that nobody seems to have noticed that AC's book called 'Moonchild' was published in 1929.[114] This was the year in which I was conceived. Knowing Crowley as well as we do, is it likely that this was pure chance? Besides, no one has remarked that the book's full title is: 'Moonchild – a Prologue'. A prologue to what? Little by little, all is falling into place.

114. The Mandrake Press, London. It was written in 1917!

16

AGNOSTOS THEOS

The Good God who is neither named nor nameless

Our Assumptions

From time to time, I introduce people to my mother. I don't make a special point of asking them *not* to shoot her! This doesn't mean that they are free to take pot-shots. It's just that the idea is so improbable that one doesn't mention it. On the other hand, if my family had been prone to assassination, I would be far more careful. But my grandmother was not mown to death on the lawn. My uncle never bit a grenade disguised as an apple. And my cousin, a milkman, never got pasteurised by mistake. So there you are, you see. I do not come from an unlucky family, nor one that is prone to accidents.

I cannot pretend to speak for the whole of Europe, but your average Englishman does not need metal underwear. The timid ones might, but only when visiting ports around the Mediterranean. Just ask your travel agent. The odds against being attacked by a madman with a shovel are minuscule. They rise by two hundred per cent in an occult bookshop! People get very incensed.

Other things are so obvious they are taken for granted. You may know me only as an author. But I wrote my first book on Crowley just three years ago. My main calling is that of occult Teacher, and I've been doing the job since I was twenty-eight years old. I am no Miss Moffat from: 'The Corn is Green'.[115] I am a Master who wanders the globe. I visit my students. There is no need for them to visit me. Between visits, I help their work

115. A very famous play by Emlyn Williams, later a film starring Bette Davies.

by sending some learning material. There are booklets, cassettes, charts and drawings. I have even come out with the odd prophecy. All in all, I work quite hard.

Yet never once, in all these years, have I ever told students that they must *not* try to castrate themselves!

I am on pretty safe ground. No one has complained about this limitation on his human rights. By the same token, no individual has jumped to the wrong conclusion. If I did not forbid the act, not one has presumed that he may make free with his chopper. I am glad that my students are not hackers off of unconsidered trifles![116] Of course, there is the odd one who has to be different. And yes, a few are overcome by strange moods from time to time. But so far this has not involved the cleaving of sexual organs, or other such gestures, more suited to Grand Opera.

The man who acted as my father for four years, Len Standish, used to smash my mother's framed photo to bits every time he got angry. He was really a coward though. He kept brand new back-ups ready in the locked drawer of his little roll-top bureau! He just liked to give us a fright. He was a very sad man and maybe even a murderer.[117]

Maleness can rouse a magical power, and semen can enter into some ritual methods. One doesn't exactly help matters by killing the goose that lays the golden eggs – or vice versa, if you follow my drift. I cannot think why an occult master might want someone to whittle away at his what's-its. I mean, you can hardly offer them as gifts. But even if I did wish someone to castrate himself then, like the Emperor of Japan, I would send him a whetted mole-trap. There would be no subtle hints. I would not pussy-foot around, I'd tell him right out. "If you wish, you may borrow the palace chain-saw." It's the only way to do it.

One gathers that the zealots of Kybele[118] were wont to do this during wilder moments of some of their revelry. They would hold a set of orgiastic rites which led to a state of frothing, demented frenzy. Then, at a precise moment, as if the Wimbledon umpire had called "New balls", they'd smash a beer-glass and tatter their

116. Autolycus, in 'The Winter's Tale', IV, ii, by Shakespeare.
117. cf. my first book: 'The Secrets of Aleister Crowley', 1991.
118. Also called Cybele, The 'Great Mother' of the Phrygians, with a cult that covered the whole of the Aegean area. She has a demonic following of ecstatic dancers, called Korybantes. Her priests were castrated.

tassels. In the heat of the moment, they probably did not realise that this gallant deed is something one can only perform once. That is to say: no one ever gets a bar to his medal for doing it twice.

In view of their condition, young men had to hang on to the evidence and produce it when required as proof. You weren't allowed to toss these things in a heap at the feet of the Goddess. You had to show that it had been a voluntary offering, freely made, and not the result of some terrible accident. I mean to say, you have seen singers, haven't you? You have noted all their erotic stances, and the indecent things they do with their guitars? Did you know that there is a gadget called a 'mandolin' that slices carrots?

You do see what I'm driving at, don't you? What sort of tragic event does all that conceal, eh?

Things Never Said

Then again, you've still got a certain kind of thief who uses scissors. In a crowded place he can reduce a man's suit to a grass skirt in one minute flat. Aleister had what he called "a very narrow escape" while he was in Egypt. Meaning to buy something from a stall he felt for the pocket in the back of his trousers. It had been replaced by a large hole – with several hands in it! "Luckily," he said simply, "at that very instant there came the call to prayers from the minarets!"

But in the days of Kybele, it wasn't enough to proffer one's genitals. One had also to flaunt the spot whence they had been plucked. The temple officers knew all about con men and cheats. A timid pilgrim could buy pairs of dried chestnuts at many a market stall. Out of season, one lured the tourists up a dark alley, and forsook them outside the town. They had the air of being quite weary and footsore or, if you prefer, knackered. This gives a whole new meaning to that famous phrase: "Come with me to the Kasbah."[119]

I exclude women from this matter, at least for the time being. With all due respect to their feminist goals, few of them have actually had the graft done. Granted that many of them look as though they already might have – built, as they are, like rugby forwards – and talking like the folk who gut fish in Aberdeen. One

---

119. Uttered by Charles Boyer into the ear of Marlene Deitrich in a film called 'The Garden of Allah'.

or two even sport the sort of moustache that would do a sergeant-major proud. I suppose one or two of them may yet ask for a new passport. When we get down to details, they'll have to stop at whiskers. 'Virilism', as this condition is called, very rarely goes all the way!

Even so, it would be a lunatic risk to kiss a nurse and say "Doctor Livingstone, I presume?"

Now there are things that AC never said either. I come across them almost every day: 1 – He never said that Israel Regardie could be 'Deputy God' on the Jewish Sabbath; 2 – He never said that Princess Margaret should refuse to give me her hand; 3 – And he never said that I should vote for women priests.

When he was raising me to be a magician, he did not appear to think that his advice was needed on any of these crucial points. This is not at all the same thing as turning a blind eye. I have loved Princess Margaret all my life and send her a Valentine card every year. I think the dear, old Duchess of York would do very well to be ordained. And since Israel Regardie has passed on, why not mount a quest to identify his 're-born form'? We might well start at the bottom of the garden.[120]

"AC never said that we should not do it!"

"AC never said it was wrong, did he?"

"If he'd wanted us to lay off, he'd have said so."

This is news to me.

There are several points in occult theory where there is no orthodox view. You are free to believe what you wish, within certain limits, to be sure. If you take the business of spirit seances, for example, then it isn't at all clear what the teaching of the Masters might be. Do they approve of your doing it, or not? Rather than live with this clouded truth, the normal student will just rely on his own opinion. This is what a Master calls 'the idiot's get-out clause', i.e., "Nobody told me I should not!"

Round and Round[121]

In many ways, the concept of the soul being born again strikes us as bizarre. That is because, in Western culture, it has never been

---

120. "There are Fairies at the bottom of our garden", from 'Fairies and Chimneys', by Rose Fyleman, 1877-1957.

121. The first line of a song that was popular in the thirties and forties: "Oh the music goes round and round, oh-oh-oh-oh, and it comes out here!"

given any specific stress. At different times the dead went to Valhalla, Niflheim, or a Lower World of some sort. The beliefs did not dwell on the chances of souls being recycled or of their being rehoused in new bodies. Even so, the concept of 'an old soul' did exist. That is to say that the arbiters of religion – Druids, Shamans, or Priests – did believe that an individual could have 'endured' for a very long time.

I don't think that they saw him as an immortal, or someone who never grew old. That is the later myth into which these beliefs were changed. They accepted that the soul was able shift to another body, by a midnight flit or by moving in together. As a matter of fact, it was thought quite possible for two persons to become one.[122] Most days, they each had a unique body, even though it might be seen as sacredly 'twinned'. But sometimes they would share the same body, and the inactive one was carefully hidden,[123] out of reach of any wandering spirits.

Now AC did not see mankind as cattle being bred on a Celestial Farm. It was not much effort to 'improve the genes' or to produce taller and more healthy types. In other words, we belong to an ancient lineage only in the sense that one lifetime gives physical being to the next. As for the soul, and the accrued wisdom of all our duration here, it is shifted from one shell to another.

The soul is like a diamond that can be moved from an ear-ring to a bracelet, or from a pendant to a tiara. The hassle is that, unlike a diamond, we can gather defects and (or) benefits during any one lifetime. In fact it rather seems that the 'noble water'[124] is being distilled. It can become as pure as the very 'elixir[125] of divinity' itself.

The oriental view of rebirth is a cyclical event that leads toward union with All or a descent into chaos. In AC's view, one's astral self advanced always along the same path. In other words, a magician has always been aligned with an occult facet in his previous lives. All men should belong to the same faith. But they do not all possess the linear quality that allows them to advance along the way.

---

122. Even the marriage ceremony, in English, speaks of man and woman being of one flesh.
123. There is an element here that entered into the vampire myth.
124. The colour or lustre of a diamond, or a pearl, is expressed in degrees of water. E.g., a diamond of the first-water is the purest known.
125. An alchemical term, probably from 'al-ihksir', a drying powder for open wounds.

I realise, of course, that this concept will go down very badly with loose and careless thinkers. They use the occult more as a hobby or a pastime. But whatever their opinions as regards this world, and the best way to run it, that has no bearing at all on outcomes in the other world. It is a weakness of reason to suppose that being 'left' or 'right' could interest the Gods. Politics is a tool made by man. Its purpose is to curb those states where the huge population breeds a type of latent violence.

I wish with all my heart there were an easy way of cleaning up the effects of lifelong bigotry in people's minds. Isn't this what the Zen Buddhist really means when he speaks of 'sartori'?[126] Isn't it just one more name for insight?

Perhaps you can at least see why our sexual nature features so much in occult beliefs. Let us leave witches on one side for the moment. We must ignore the perverts who use the occult to conceal their sick minds. Our best moments of ecstasy, when the 'self' is eclipsed by some larger being, are reached when we shrug off our mental fetters. It seems quite sound and reasonable to us that we may indeed seek access to the Gods via the avenue of creative power. Indeed, this is why so many 'new'[127] beliefs went out of their way to condemn it and impose a ruthless morality. The men who manage religion have to come to some agreement with the men who deal in political power. This is their undoing. Let politics take care of Caesar's goals; let religion take care of God's.

Vampires

I know why young folk have an avid interest in 'past lives' and why there is a thriving market for accessories. Some groups focus only on 'reading' past lives! The only value is that it supports the view that one does possess a spirit. It is not proof. It would be more valuable to know what one's next life might be. You could then get yourself ready. I know a man who has always been associated with the Slavonic peoples. This excites him deeply, but I try to help him find his destiny rather than his

---

126. Instant or slow realisation of truth.
127. New in the sense that Christianity and Islam and many, many sects are new in comparison with the age of mankind. New also in the sense that the majority of modern religions have been 'founded' by a single individual who was himself something of a social rebel.

history. My friend would do better to be a new Kyril or Methodius.[128] He has the makings of a 'khlysti' or Slavonic Holy Man.

When someone 'burns' with zeal for this or that metier, then he probably feels a magical stimulus. I don't mean that juvenile longing to be best, to get a golden disk, or to rise above the common herd. I am speaking of a 'divine madness', which was known to Isadora Duncan, Mozart, Van Gogh and Leonardo da Vinci. "Genius is close to madness", says the old maxim. More than that, they are twins ... but one of them limps.

This brings me to the question of the Vampire – one of those global myths. Indeed, there are so many versions on the theme that it's a problem sorting them all out. But the things they all have in common are these:

1. They are not 'living' in the normal accepted meaning of the word. Either they are dead souls who return or some sort of half-way soul that is neither dead nor alive. Hence that paradox about 'the living dead' which, if you analyse it, means pure drivel.

2. They are all trying to steal some fluid or essence from live victims. This is often blood, but it has also been semen, 'life force', or the 'vital energy'.

If we examine the alchemy of, say, Gilles de Rais, the concept of 'the elixir of life' was never as prosaic as folk imagine. Both AC and I believe that certain human beings are what used to be labelled 'vampires' or 'werewolfs'. You probably know one or two yourselves. They drain your vital energy.

This is not the moment to talk about garlic, holy water, or crosses and stakes through the heart. All are ways of turning vampires into pet food. You see, there is an older tradition that being 'thrown to the dogs' destroys all life force and ends further rebirth. Notice how Shakespeare spoke of "the dogs of war" in Julius Caesar. Remember myths, such as "Herm the Hunter" in Windsor Great Park, along with his "pack of hell-hounds". Finally, notice which of the Egyptian gods had the heads of dogs or jackals, and why.

Is a dog truly man's best friend? It wasn't always so!

---

128. The two saints sent by the Orthodox Church to act as missionaries to the Slavs. It is reputed that St.Cyril invented the alphabet which is still in use and called 'Cyrillic' in his honour. He died c.869.

17
THANATOS

The Son of Night and the Brother of Sleep

Grief

After AC died, life went on.

I was sorry that they chose to cremate him. Myself, I would have liked to have a tomb to visit. They do their best, I know. But when they cremate someone, there isn't the same dignity, and it can't be called a proper funeral. For one thing, of course, one has to leave before they've finished doing whatever they do. So one has a slight feeling of things being left hanging, so to speak, in the air. For another thing, it is all a bit too quick. There are plenty of churches about, aren't there? That means there are plenty of parsons happy to lay on a full, one-hour funeral, with or without choir, organ and tolling bell. You have time to adjust – time to adapt yourself to the idea that he or she has gone.

There may be only the one facility within miles. They have to use a computer just to track the fifteen minute slots given to this or that funeral director. You have to be there – on the dot! You have to be out again – on the dot. If you're lucky, you won't see your floral tributes being dragged away to make room for the next lot. This heavy stress on being timely is quite foreign to the tried ways of a funeral director. They are skilful people, when all's said and done, but their standards are ruffled by this need for a stopwatch. You might almost imagine that there are opposing teams back there, behind the scenes. Is there an amazing bonus to be gained by the team that can shift the largest number of corpses per shift?

The result is that the cortège of cars hurtles through the streets like a scene from a silent movie. Flowers are lost at every corner one takes. You can see the coffin rocking and you pray to God that he won't have to slam his brakes on suddenly, lest the deceased should arrive first. Grandad is looking so blue and bleary, you question the wisdom of taking him home again after. You get there like people who missed the Titanic. You're whisked in, the coffin edges off-stage, you catch a brief glimpse of a chaplain, and then you're whisked out again. It is very much like Gatwick airport really. They try to get you out of 'departures' before you catch sight of the hearses sweeping in to 'arrivals'.

You're not quite sure what it is you've been to. But whatever it was, it is now over. You are left there, cold, tense, with your grief still not allayed. In England, you know, one is not allowed to purge one's grief. In warmer climes, a funeral is not a funeral unless one shrieks and froths at the mouth. But as you go North, toward the colder climes, the public displays of grief become more and more subdued. We go in for more dignity, we think. In Finland, I wouldn't wonder, they all turn their backs and push them down a ski-slope into a sea of nuclear fuel. When it is frozen, they go sliding across the ice like the Scottish game of curling.

What does Ecology say, I wonder? An old Yorkshire song, 'On Ilkley Moor', explains how those who die will be scoffed by worms. After that though, the worms will be gobbled up by ducks. Then we come and eat up the ducks. So it is only logical to confess that we have all eaten each other. Quite a sensible idea, come to think of it. It's enough to turn anyone 'Green'.

If we're going to cremate our dead, for whatever reason, then let's do it like Ancient Greeks or the Vikings. Let us build royal pyres. Let us push burning boats out into the sea. Let us shriek, for heaven's sake, and let us rip our funeral clothes to shreds. We would feel much better, wouldn't we? Far more sensible than keeping it all bottled up inside. Did you know that the death of a beloved is just about the greatest tension that the human organism can undergo? You need to grieve. You need to adapt your whole system to a world in which a loved one is missing. If you don't adapt, you will 'die a little' yourself.

What Remains?
To visit a grave. To pay homage at the spot where someone fell in battle. Or even to put flowers at the spot where a fatal accident

took place. These things purge our grief that little bit more capably. It is no loss of dignity to weep! It is not indecent to show your heart. We need a focus though. We need a point at which our fingers might just touch. What better place than where we last drew apart? There, at the side of the grave, where we say our last farewell.

I don't care how truly one tries. A quiet, pensive stroll through a Garden of Rest does not fill the bill. You have no focus, you see. To be utterly truthful, you're a wee bit nervous about the nature of the mud on your boots. His ashes have been strewn, along with an unknown number of others. You're a mite uneasy about the greenness of the lawn, and the evident vigour of the hedges.

There is no true sense of presence either. You do not truly 'feel' that this is where contact exists between the two worlds. Now I do not myself go along with Catholic belief. I do not believe that, during the Mass, bread and wine secretly change into the material of Christ's blood and body.[129] But millions of quite honest people do and, what is more, they derive immense comfort from doing so. To compare a grave with the lawn where one scatters ashes, is like going from the basilica to a bus-stop. It all comes down to a sense of presence, you see. Have you come to whimper about a loss that's still hurting, or have you called by to update your scrap-book?

But had they buried AC, his remains would not have been safe. There are no lengths to which outraged members of a church will not go to vent their tantrums of wrath. Thugs would have defaced his tomb. Hoodlums would have broken it. Even deranged fans from other paths would have rifled it for relics. Did you know that a secret source sold the alleged 'penis' of Napoleon Bonaparte at a London auction in 1972? If they had not cremated AC, there would now be a thriving black market in his bones, if nothing more intimate.

I, and others like me, we would have trodden softly. We would have paid homage and sought peace for our spirits. But others though, they would have come to dance in contempt and commit impiety. No, I do not blame them for burning his body and strewing his ashes to the wind. As it is, there is a regular theft of soil. They smuggle it out in handfuls and, if you know where to go, you can purchase tiny amounts of it in central London.

129. The doctrine of transubstantiation.

"During my life," he said, "I have been liberal, not to say prodigal, with certain parts of my anatomy. After I am dead, I would like them to rest! One can never be certain if one might not need them again!" I had recently read a black magic novel by Dennis Wheatley. In it, the goodies and baddies were vying with each other to get custody of the phallus of Thoth. "Had they but come to me," he murmured, "I would have been quite happy to share it between them."

I missed him, but not perhaps as much as you think I ought. I had no urge to commit suttee.[130] Neither did I feel like tearing out my teeth and gnashing my hair – or is it be the other way round? I even dismayed myself at how little emotion I felt. It wasn't a stiff upper lip, so typical of the English; it was a total absence of grief. I felt guilty as if I were failing in my duty and letting him down. Now I realize it was a normal sort of inner conflict for a youth of my age. At the time though, I didn't know what was expected when one lost one's father.

Mourning

I never went to my sister's funeral either. They wouldn't let me because I was only four. After that, the only other death I'd known was a young aunt and I remember her funeral vividly. While the rest of the family were taciturn and properly drained of colour, my buffoon of an uncle had a field day. He howled, sobbed, tore his shirt buttons off, and banged his head against a wall which was densely covered in ivy. There being no TV then, mourners from other funerals came across to see the show. When finally her coffin was lowered into the ground, he tried to throw himself into the grave.

"Leave him be," said grandma. "It's too late," she sniffed tersely. "He never once told her that he loved her. So let him scream it from the bloody roof-tops – she'll not hear!"

Her own grief was a slight redness of the eye, and a greyish green tinge to her cheeks. Her hand trembled when she sipped some sherry at the usual funeral tea!

I don't know what I felt as regards AC. It was a very odd affair. I met him when I was already seven and we parted when I was only fourteen. Yes, I liked him and there was fondness, but I just

130. In India, wives used to fling themselves into their husbands funeral fires. The British tried to stop the custom but never quite succeeded.

can't say whether it counted as love. He never implied such a thing himself and I don't think he hoped for it. It is only now, as I grow old, that I discern my emotion and know its strength. I felt a gentle awe.

Judging by the films I had seen, and the grand opera that I was starting to enjoy, I should have felt lost, bereft and burst into an aria. But I didn't. I thought I'd got the measure of the old man. I felt that I knew what made him tick. Never for a moment would he be content to pack his bags and go wherever they sent him. If the decision were his, he'd be back at the first occasion and make his presence felt!

Which is exactly what he did.[131]

It was not a stately death but it would have been if he'd planned it. If he'd had any choice in the matter it would have been grand theatre. He'd have clutched the curtains, bumped into the scenery, tottered to centre stage – and died the death of a Caesar!

As for my mother, with all her love of the silent films, one might have expected her to repeat the stunning visit that Nazimova paid to the bier of Rudolf Valentino. But she kept her head and took the news quietly. But oh, what an actress she has been in her day! Lillian Gish, Bette Davis and Greta Garbo all rolled into one. You may have seen one of the many versions of 'Anna Karenina' that exist. They are as nothing compared to what my own, dear mother has been playing all her life. What superb exits we have had, what calm stoicism, what swoons, smiles and gay reunions! Each flimsy, tight telegram nailed to numb bosoms. All those tender, scented swoons in dramas of love! And more, much more than this, the doors she has closed quietly, but with the resonant boom of the gates of hell.

With parents like that, I do sometimes feel that perhaps I was meant to be one of the living legends. Instead of which, my name is in the tiniest print on the reverse of the programme: "solo flute, AC Junior". I have not made enough noise. The gang which follows AC today cherish people who kick up a stink. They're not too bad at it, in their own right. Since their own Master's dead, they have to make a racket. You can see how it is. Kindling up zeal can be a bit tricky when not much happens any more.

131. See the previous chapter for quotations gleaned at a spirit seance.

Granted, when you join, the papers you receive, and the mystical jargon you have to learn, must seem quite imposing. "Good Golly, Miss Molly," you all but sing, "this stuff is deep, d-e-e-p, D-E-E-P!" Kids get the same thrills when you buy them one of these new modelling kits. You know the sort, with a sordid replica of the monster from 'Alien'. Then they do it as easy as pie. No snag at all. What is more, once it has been done, it's totally without any known use.

Emissaries

If you have genuine faith in these occult orders – if it's more than zeal, but burning passion – then stop reading. I don't want to upset you. Pop your free-will in the gas oven and your brain in the deep-freeze. Better still: stay in your joint coma. If you never know what you missed, you'll have no need to grieve. That's how it is with some types of mental illness. In view of what they suffered in the past, some patients are better off being mad.

To be quite honest, during my tenure of office, I have never attacked nor insulted any occult order. I used to see them with different eyes. I assumed they were doing good work for the rest of humanity. After my first book was published, they seemed a bit worried. They didn't like what I had to say nor the language in which I couched it. Some of them took it as a direct warning. To cut a long story short, they began verbally to attack me!

Occult Law forbids me to harm others deliberately. But I am not expected to bare my neck and lay it on the block. As in certain of the 'martial arts' that grew out of Buddhism, I may turn a person's hostility against him. In this sense, at least, we are all standing on the brink of an occult war. I have asked for peace, but to no avail. Rather than concede a single point, some occultists would rather die. These are the lengths to which pride will lead men. I won't argue. I shall now string my bow.

I met the agents of one occult group. I applaud their courage for having contacted me. One of their leaders wanted a special reward for his years of experience. He expected a special prize for 'turning' to me. The situation was like the meeting between Jesus and Simon Magus. I offered him knowledge but he wanted a feather in his hat. I could have given him truth, but he wanted status. He must admit: it would have been so easy to say "yes".

He must realize that it was purely my conscience which made me say "no".

Do you demand a seat in the choir of angels? Is it reasonable to sulk in front of the Gods? This is the ultimate insanity, to believe that you are an irreplaceable piece in a cosmic game of chess. He tried to put pressure on me. He would acknowledge me as Master if I would recognize his worth. But I am a Master and no one's 'yeah' or 'nay' affects that. To accept me or reject me is a person's free choice, and he is the one most affected. I am not here to solicit votes. There is nothing democratic about the Gods. That man knew only what he *wanted*. He had no idea what he might *need*.

It is a shame that occultists have to spend so much of their time and energy on guarding themselves against other occultists. It's almost like politics, isn't it? One seems to attract enemies without ever wishing to. So far they haven't attacked me in any physical way. They have not used magic. But they give me the cold shoulder – or is that all that they have? They treat me as if I were an Egyptian mummy who forgot to change his bandages.

But I am confident that things will change. To make quite sure of that, I have actually decided to change them. The game's afoot and the bird is on the wing. I shall now go a-hunting for a change. They say I have a touch of theatre and a great sense of timing. I know when to pause, and let that pause speak volumes. So did Shakespeare it seems. Just four words that say so much ... "The rest is silence."[132]

132. Hamlet, Act V. sc ii.

18

'ATTAR

In South Arabia, he was the God of War and Battle

No Memorial[133]

There are certain people, a handful in each country perhaps, who together possess the greatest power in the modern world. They are members of a group. This group does not have many Generals, Presidents, Directors or Bankers on its lists. It has them in its pockets. This group has been shaping the face of Europe for many centuries. Now, of course, it is able to manipulate the whole world and modify our destiny. I do not say this merely to grab your attention. I say it because it is true.

I assume that you are at least as sensible as me. I know that what I have just said sounds more like a James Bond novel than a book about Occultism. Strangely enough, I think that James Bond, or his inventor, would endorse all that I say. This is the why there is a certain resonance between his books and mine. He did give hints, you remember. He knew about these things.

Just for once, I am not talking about the Freemasons. I think they would welcome that sort of publicity. If they don't actually say it, at least they never deny that they are the world's most powerful secret society. But it is not true, and we must not turn their heads. To be quite frank, Freemasonry just isn't up to it. They are not even in the running. I would never let my daughter marry a Freemason, and I would never buy a second-hand car from one. But my personal feelings don't enter in to it. Jah-Bul-On[134] is not

---

133. "And some there be, which have no memorial". The Bible, Ecclesiasticus 44.9.
134. The name they attribute to 'The Great Architect of the Universe', but actually a 'compound deity' formed of three distinct beings: Jah = Jhvh, or Jehovah, the God claimed by the Jews. Bul = The ancient fertility God, Baal, who is usually associated with certain sexual excesses. On = Osiris, or the God of the Underworld at the time of the Pharaohs.

all that he's cracked out to be. As Sherlock Holmes said: "Use the knee-jerk test!"

The Freemasons claim they are not a secret society. Yes, and Hitler said he was liberating Poland. But we must take their word for it. One wonders then why they take such dreadful oaths of secrecy. "Do they want it both ways?" Aleister would have asked, blinking innocently. "Then what is the point of pretending to be virgins?" I also wonder why certain books are banned? And why did they make jubilee when Stephen Knight died?[135]

I have an interest in the matter. 'The Hermetic Order of the Gold Dawn' and 'The Ordo Templi Orientis' were both born under the aegis of Freemasonry. It was one of their tiny social experiments – like letting women in to certain lodges but keeping them second class citizens. Very much like a synagogue, when you come to think of it. But I must waste less time on those amusing Masons. I wish I could persuade them to stop pulling the wool over their own eyes.

You do realize, gentleman, that your aprons and other regalia will not go with you, beyond the grave? All the privilege that you solicit here and now, will be denied you there and then. If truth were told, you don't even believe that you've got it all sewn up. It's amusing. It brings privileges. But there will be a price.[136]

My Name is Legion[137]

The group of which I spoke at the opening of this chapter, is not a household name. Come to that, it takes great care never to be highly visible. It had to be good, to hide from the journalists of the tabloid press. But could one start an investigation? In the whole of Great Britain, there are only three of these chaps. In Ireland there are two. In France there are eight. In Germany there are six. In the whole of America, north and south, there are twenty.

Forget about your liturgy and your solemn oaths. These men are so wealthy – so uniquely rich – they can get round all security that there is. They have their agents in the Masons, the

---

135. Michael Short, 'Inside the Brotherhood', Grafton Books, 1991.
136. For all ex-brothers, and all those brothers who wish they were ex, I should be glad to 'untie' your abominable oaths and to decontaminate you, so to speak. Just contact me via my publishers.
137. "My Name is Legion: for we are many." St.Mark 5:9. Words attributed to the Devil.

Rosicrucians and any secret society of any concern at all. Even The Priory of Sion lies in their field of control. Needless to say, The United States of America is one of their favourite toys.

These people can bring their influence to bear in any elected body, among jurists, and in any kind of council. They 'possess' a few of the key men at the highest levels of the EEC. They have four of their own pets in crucial posts in the Vatican. They have agents in every political party and trade union. They do not much bother about any form of ideology.[138] They operate at a much higher level, which is why we find it difficult to perceive their actions. They distract the average man by giving him the right wing and the left wing to quarrel about. They have great skill in the art of metapolitics, i.e., dealing with affairs on a global scale.

So you see, all our statesmen play minor roles in a much larger scenario. As long as we are kept busy with our low level debate, they are just digging in deeper. It doesn't even matter which 'colour' of governments we elect – all of them will carry out the policies of these other, hidden power brokers. On the surface, you may 'see' a great deal of difference between the acts of one government and the policies of another one. But under the stealth, it is their wishes that are carried out.

It really is quite simple, when you think about it. Even in quite recent years, we have all seen what a fall on the Stock Markets can do. If need be, any specific company can be made bankrupt, and any big shot can be ruined. Look what they did to the giant American air lines. Look what they did to Robert Maxwell.[139] Can you imagine the outcome if this sort of thing happened to IBM, Sony, or a similar business in any of the western states? "What about state economy?" you might ask. That is my point precisely – what *about* state economy?

A few of you, the more cunning, might even grimace and ask about war. Yes, you guessed it. These few persons are the arbiters of war, the angels of death, and the fathers of famine. They are the ones behind crowning, regicide, coups d'etat and the whole of

---

138. i.e., political or religious belief.
139. I have reason to believe that Robert Maxwell is not dead. The well-planned 'accident' has convinced most people. But the local magistrates did their work very swiftly and the Israeli government gave him a state funeral very quickly. Now that Czechoslovakia is about to split up, a certain wealthy land-owner may have to be 'displaced' yet again.

world trade. Peace be unto Madame Blavatsky,[140] but these are the real, the only hidden masters. In a certain sense, these are the real Lords of Power.

Sand in the Wind[141]

Naturally, with all the power they possess, they have gone to great lengths to hide their identity, their action and even their existence. They have thought of most of the risky possibilities and they have long since planned their defensive measures.

For example, they have seen to it that a certain idea has been well and truly grafted on to most of your minds. Has it never struck you? If anyone, anywhere, raises the cry of "wolf", your first reaction (along with that of writers, reporters and any other human being) is to assume that he is cracked. You do it routinely as if your brain had been 'set' like an alarm clock. If he talks like that, then it is obvious he is mad. You've seen films though, haven't you? What I have in mind is the old classics, such as 'The Invaders' and stuff of that sort. The people I'm talking about helped in the making of those films. In a sideways manner, they invested some of their own money when lots of other backers were wary. They would be delighted if you treat this chapter as a joke or a piece of fantasy.

Pardon me but very few people are qualified to say whether I am mentally ill. If you imply that I am cracked, I do not lose sleep. You have been trained to react the way you do. When you respond to that training, you do it by reflex. You mean it. Just like the people who shot President Kennedy. It is quite true though. Many people who found out the facts have ended up in clinics and hospitals. Good God, why are you so surprised? Soviet Russia did it. Red China still does it. Why do you resist the idea that it could be happening here – and in America?

Are you able to be objective enough to give a fair reading to a theory I could put on the table? Do you have the mental strength to examine it *before* you chuck it out? Humour me for a moment. Here's the proposition: what if you are wrong and I am right? Do you see what I'm driving at? Is it wise to nibble canapes with such

140. Madame Helena Petrovna Blavatsky, 1831-1891: often regarded as the founder of modern occultism. She was also the founder of the Theosophical Society.
141. William Blake, MS Notebooks: "Mock on, mock on Voltaire, Rousseau; Mock on, mock on, 'tis all in vain! You throw sand against the wind, and the wind blows it back again."

a strong smell of smoke about? Isn't it foolish to fiddle when someone is crying "fire!"? You laugh and do nothing. But if you took me at my word, there is so little that you stand to lose. Does it matter how remote the possibility might be? If there's a chance that you might just save the world – all it will cost is one bite of the apple. Not such bad odds, eh?

Instead of just flinging scorn at me, why not start to ask questions? You have nothing at all to lose. So dig deep. Light up the darkest corners of your mind and have a good look round. What is it that makes you routinely resist my claim? Your training! You don't think for yourself, you push a button and you obey the signals. Who then is driving your train?

You, and millions like you, have all the right symptoms of 'The Day of Doom Syndrome'. That is my own title for the sort of conduct you display. I, or someone like me, tries to warn you of an imminent danger. What do you do? You want to smile. You feel some pity. You are a wee bit coy. I call it 'The Day of Doom Syndrome' because of those pathetic men who brandish rainy banners which proclaim "The End is Nigh". "Repent! Repent!" they beg you. "Before God lets loose His terrible judgement."

I feel like one of those men. Except that I accept the sheer futility of ever telling you about it. You will not thank me. You will not change your life. You will just step aside and avoid me.

But ... what if I'm right?

A Blaze of Riot[142]
In fact, we use the expression – "a prophet of doom" – to mean someone whose dire warnings never come to pass. They said it too often. Even when scientists talk about 'ozone layer', 'greenhouse effect' or 'global warming', we tend not to prick up our ears. Land can become desert. Rivers can pollute. Sunrays can cause cancer. You react to the words, and only certain words will make you listen. Others make you snort with derision. None of which alters the facts. If the Day of Doom *is* nigh, then it is nigh.

"So what?" you might then sneer. "There's nothing I can do about it." Why would you say that? If there was a forest fire, you'd have a go. If there were terrible floods, you'd not hesitate to wade out and rescue folk. Isn't it all part of *being human* that we

---

142. Shakespeare, Richard II. "Methinks I am a prophet new inspir'd, and thus expiring do foretell of him: His rash fierce blaze of riot cannot last..."

guard our hopes? In spite of all the things that ought to cause despair – like the children of Yugoslavia – we manage to run.

So why are you ready to throw in the sponge when one talks of the Day of Doom? It can hardly be that your minds are crippled by the sheer enormity of the event. To be quite honest, I doubt if many people can even take that in. Just as some people have an aptitude for suicide, so you have been prepared to be negative about the end. In other words, my dear brothers, it is not I who am mad ... it is you who have been got at.

Let's face facts. For the past few thousand years, mankind has been winding down! Look at the 'Pax Romana'; see the epoch of Spanish grandeur; think of the British Empire. All of them were bogus appeals to patriotism. Second only to religion, patriotism has been a major cause of death, worse even than any plague. But at the same time, one small group has always come out well.

It was all well and good for King Henry V to give the great war cry "God for Harry, England and Saint George!" Henry V ate meat every day off gold plates. "Vive la France!" is another good motto. It has led millions of Frenchmen to their death. Think of all the other phrases: Friends, Romans, Comrades, – Lads.

Quick! King-Kong is loose!

Have you seen one of those films where a character runs into town, dashes into a bar, and shouts: "Listen! There's a crack in the dam." No one believes him. The good-time girl says, "Forget it Harry, and give me a kiss." The barman says, "Take the weight off you feet and have a beer." The sheriff shoves a cheroot in his mouth. "Take it easy, boy. We don't want to start a panic." The pianist plays. The laughter resumes. And we all watch the floor getting wetter ... and wetter.

It's the same type of reaction with any unexpected news. "The Martians have landed," is as hilarious as "There's a crocodile in the sewers!" They are going to laugh. They think it's as unlikely as Israel and Ireland joining forces to invade Cuba. It is so unlikely – it falls into the realm of the absurd.

Sitting in the cinema, the audience is gripped. They can't wait for those stupid grins to be wiped off the characters' faces. We know something they don't. We have seen the same thing that the hero saw. We want these fools to get their come-uppance. Wait till the comet crashes through the roof, or the crocodile starts snapping knackers off! These puny, lesser beings will see how we and the hero bask in the grandeur of Gods.

Of course, if we had missed that one, short, all-important scene – then we too would behave as daft as them. What if we didn't know what he knows? What if we weren't in on it? Well, then we'd be among the sceptics, and when the catastrophe struck, we'd go under. *That is what is happening.* I have seen it. You have not. You mock and they have a sardonic gleam in the eye. They think they are going to win.

Where Angels Dwell[143]

The national press of a country has an interest in news, scandal and, at times, precision. So they held a poll among angels, at their own expense. They kept it simple. They didn't divide the sample population into sub-groups like Thrones, Powers, Cherubin and Seraphim. They used the mass approach. They dealt with them en bloc. Quite simply, they invited each one to say what it was like, being a messenger of God. The results were startling. Not one angel enjoyed his job. Each had already asked for a transfer.

This research may be new to you. But you can see why morale was low. When they said what they had been sent to say, nobody believed them either. "I am Gabriel," they vowed, or "I am Raphael", as the case might be. The most common response was, "Pull the other one!" This was not how the Virgin Mary reacted when told that she was pregnant! This is not what the Prophet Mahomet said when they brought him the Koran. Nor was it what AC said when faced with the demon, Choronzon. Not that it would have made any difference. I mention it to show that things aren't what they used to be. God's heralds were once very highly respected.[144] But so were policeman. Today, we are blasé.

If angels used the telephone, we might listen. How much more difficult it is for a plain, workaday prophet. We go out of our way to give due warning, and hardly anyone listens.

"Why didn't you make them believe you?" God will ask.

"We tried, but they said they knew better."

143. Voltaire, 1764, Philosophical Dictionary. "It is not known precisely where angels dwell – whether in the air, the void or the planets. It has not been God's pleasure that we should be informed of their abode."

144. "Be not forgetful to entertain strangers: for thereby some have entertained angels unawares." Hebrews 13:2

19

MARUTS

The seven storm-gods born to Diti, who sought to revenge herself against Indra for hurting her elder sons

Wars and Rumours of Wars

In the United States of America, at the eastern tip of Long Island, sits Montauk Point. Just to the west of it is a derelict Air Force Base.[145] During World War II, this base was used to develop the 'Rainbow Project'. Basically, the idea was either (a) to cover American ships with an electro-magnetic shield, or (b) to enclose them in an electro-magnetic 'bottle'. The object, in either case, was to render a ship 'invisible' to enemy radar. These experiments resulted in the 'Philadelphia Experiment', which has been the subject of a Hollywood film.

Briefly, a trial took place in 1943 but, as some of the scientists had feared, something went terribly wrong. The American ship, USS Eldridge, simply vanished in front of everyone's eyes. It shifted about four hundred miles to the south, and appeared instantaneously near Norfolk, Virginia. Then the reverse happened and the ship 'came back'. When it was boarded, they found that many members of the ship's crew were embedded in the metal structures, or even 'merged' with fixtures. Those who had escaped this pitiable state were in a state of total, mental horror. Some of them were mad.

The survivors were discharged and underwent years of psychiatric treatment. They were also given 'new' identities. In some cases, this treatment did not do much to help resettle people

---

145. This itself was situated on an army base dating back to the First World War and known as 'Fort Hero'.

in civilian life. In all cases, it appears to have wiped out large chunks of memory. One or two of these unfortunate individuals have tried to tell their story to newspapers, to radio journalists, or even to authors who might write a book on their behalf. But the history of 'psychiatric illness', or the diagnosis of 'psychotic' made sure that none of these stories was ever taken seriously. Certainly, they were not believed.

This is not a story that I have made up. It is not science fiction. The story has been told[146] by an electrical engineer, named Preston Nichols, and his associate, Peter Moon. It is significant that the joint authors feel it necessary to make a prominent disclaimer, behind the title page. They state that nothing in the book is intended as an attack on the government of the United States. There are solid reasons for believing that this unusual step was essential.

Mr Nichols began working for a well-known defence contractor in 1971. One of the topics he studied was the possibility that telepathy worked on principles similar to radio waves. Finding that this was indeed the case, he made tests on a large sample of 'psychics', first ensuring that they did indeed possess genuine gifts.[147] To his utter astonishment, he learned that each and every one of them suffered a 'black-out' at the same time every day. Their telepathic abilities were simply 'jammed' for a period of twenty minutes.

This was so extremely odd that Mr Nichols felt compelled to find the cause. In 1974, he set up his instruments at several locations, on the same principle as a 'direction finder'. Lo and behold, he found a powerful emission of a 410-420 MHz cycle which he was able to track direct to Montauk Point. The base which had been closed down by the government at the end of the war, had been re-opened by someone else in 1969.

It appears that this installation was being used without the knowledge of the US government, and therefore without its permission. Having interested a US Senator, officials probed

146. P.B. Nichols and P. Moon, 'The Montauk Project: Experiments in Time', Sky Books, 1992. ISBN 0-9631889-0-9

147. Science has now accepted that such things do exist, and they would normally be studied by a parapsychologist. In this case, though, Mr Nichols was not studying the phenomena of telepathy. He was researching the means by which the telepaths received or sent their messages.

every single department without success. No one has yet been able to locate the source of the funds, nor identify the group that invested so much money and personnel.

A Monstrous Presence

Naturally, Mr Nichols felt a certain compulsion to visit the 'disused' base. When he got to the site, he found it crawling with security personnel whose insignia, on shoulders and caps, were unlike any he had ever seen. They turned him away firmly, simply saying that hush-hush experiments were taking place. Before he left, Mr Nichols noticed a red and white radar reflector sitting on top of one of the buildings. It was clear why they had not attempted to hide it: It was almost as long a football field!

Ten years later, in 1984, a friend telephoned Mr Nichols to say that the base really was abandoned now. Together they visited the site again. There were signs of some sort of catastrophe and of a hurried departure. Most interesting of all, there were tons electronic equipment which Mr Nichols found intriguing. He contacted the agency which dealt with the disposal of army surplus, but they didn't know what he was talking about. In the end, he found a Colonel who told him that the base belonged to the government, but they knew nothing about the equipment. He was free to take what he wanted.

When they visited the site again, they found an elderly caretaker who was very reluctant to let them in. The Colonel had given them a 'note' which was far from official, and so the old man told them they could look round this one time. He added, no doubt for their benefit, that he went for his evening meal at seven p.m.

Nichols and his friend searched everywhere. They found 'standing orders' and 'daily bulletins' still pinned to notice boards. In an office they found copies of regular discharge papers for several 'army' personnel. Nichols also stumbled on an old tramp, dossing down in a remote out-building. The man appeared to recognize Nichols. It seemed that he had worked at this base, and that Nichols had been his boss!

There was a distinct air of secrecy about the base, and over the years since the war, it has given birth to many legends among the people of Long Island. But as is often the case, truth is stranger than fiction. People who are 'in the know' have excellent reasons for believing that this affair, now dubbed the 'Montauk Project', was a continuation of those earlier, war-time experiments. Research had been going on for thirty years, and the precise objective had been (a) electronic mind surveillance, and (b) population control within given areas.

In 1983, forty years exactly since the 'Philadelphia Experiment', the experiments once again went awry. Somehow or other, the scientists tore a hole in the space-time continuum. Not only did it loop back forty years, but it probably 'bulged' in other directions because 'something monstrous' came through the tunnel. So far as is known, it may still be living there, at Montauk Point.

A Link Back

Mr Nichols' story gets more and more interesting. Other people recognize him and talk of the old days. In his department, where he worked for a giant defence contractor, plasters and wound dressings would appear and disappear from his hands. On one occasion he wandered down into a sub-level and found his own name on a door, designating him as assistant project director.

It eventually transpired that his mind had been manipulated, and that one 'person' still worked on a secret project, while another 'person' enacted the role of P. B. Nichols. The climax came when these two aspects of his own being, living, so to speak, on different time streams, began to recognize each other. His resignation from the job was accepted – no one had realized the extent to which his mind was recovering, and he has since contacted many other people in a similar position. Their organization has constructed 'Space-Time Laboratories' in several places.

The co-author, Peter Moon, read my first book, and wrote to me. Why? Ah that is the point that I need to develop carefully. At face value, there doesn't seem to be anything to connect a 'scientific project' with AC, myself, or occultism. Except that AC visited Montauk Point and camped there, in a tent, during the summer of 1918, when he was thirty-three years old. There is also evidence that in the 1800s the author's family and the Crowley family invested in the first electronics company in Great Britain. It appears that this has since developed into Thorn EMI. There is a rumour that Thorn EMI helped to finance the film, 'Philadelphia Experiment', and also distributed it. In that film, there was material that could only have been known by an insider.

I must now take you back a little earlier, to the arrival in the USA of a Dr Wilhelm Reich, who was fleeing from the Fascists. In the USA in 1940 the government launched a project whose purpose was to control weather. It was known as 'Phoenix', and its basic principles and technology came from Reich. But while they accepted and used Reich's theories, they heartily disapproved of the man himself. It ended with the prosecution of Reich, a long prison sentence and the destruction of all his equipment and notes.

Wilhelm Reich is well-known to young people for his views on the value of sex on a spiritual plane. He suggested a form of energy which he called 'orgone', and constructed many devices which purported to help people who were charged with 'dead orgone'. Is there not a clear parallel here with the views of AC, and my own teachings? I do not believe for an instant that Reich influenced Crowley. What I do believe is that both men (and others) reach very similar conclusions via different routes.

One thing more … Wilhelm Reich claimed to have developed a means that could jam the 'drives' of UFOs!

Jumping Jack

The electro-magnetic bottle, which had been the object of Project Rainbow, combined with the results of Project Phoenix, have brought about today's 'stealth aircraft'. The original 'combined' work was headed by Dr John von Neumann, a Hungarian scientist who built the first vacuum-tube computer at Princetown University. In his attempts to grapple with the 'metaphysical' concept of a human spirit or soul, he found that this aspect of a human being is an 'energy being' to whom there is attached a sort of 'time-point', i.e., a reference point in the time-space continuum.

There is no point in my attempting to explain these theories in any depth. But von Neumann, who consulted Einstein frequently, realized that if a person were to be enclosed in an 'electro-magnetic bottle', then his being would be detached from his time-space reference point. When, and if, one got him out of the bottle, what would he have experienced, and what would he perceive as reality?

The project was completed in 1967 and a report was submitted to the US Congress for further financing. This was refused. The project was ordered to be closed down. In 1969 final orders were issued to disband the research team and to dispose of all documents and technology.

But someone seems to have picked up the project and to have continued paying for it. They kept it going until 1983, i.e., for fourteen more years – and the fortieth anniversary of the Philadelphia Incident. Who might this person or organisation have been? My own suggestion is – the persons I spoke about in Chapter 18. What shall we call them ... The Overlords of Chaos, perhaps?

Despite the opinions of the magazine, Chaos International, I am something other than a fake, a fraud, or a destroyer of young persons. In my first book,[148] I declare, quite openly, that I have altered dates and places to avoid being identified. But who was it that I didn't wish to identify me? In fact, I didn't want to provide the information from which my 'time-space' reference point could be calculated – and thence, to have my own 'reality' interfered with. You can understand that, can't you?

But this is one of those problems that one can resolve, given patience and resources. They, these Overlords of Chaos, are carrying out lengthy experiments to pin-point the details of my birth. This is why I am so often, so close to calamity and potential death. I cannot say whether they were getting close to my space grid (where I was born) or the exact moment of my birth (the time grid). All I can tell you is that they won't find me by using a computer, or by a process of elimination. On three occasions, I have been 'helped' by means of a slight adjustment of that time-space reference point: 1. At the age of thirteen;[149] 2. At my initiation;[150] 3. At my designation on the moors.[151]

If you ponder the question a little more deeply, you will also realise that the 'monster' which apparently came through the 'tunnel' to stay at Montauk Point, does not seem all that different from those captivating entities which I describe as "my astral Rottweilers".

---

148. 'The Secrets of Aleister Crowley'.
149. ibid, Chapter 22.
150. ibid Chapter 23.
151. cf. this book, Chapter 14.

20

OLORUN

A Voodoo God with neither temple nor priests

The Smoke-Screen

The first thing I must try to put across is that there is a new aspect on occultism these days. They way that people have been interpreting things, and reading the symbols, has been undergoing a profound change. The members of the Old School are terribly loath even to consider the propositions. One presumes that, like the dinosaur, they will become extinct.

To be quite precise, I, and others like me, have been teaching that the traditional, stereotype view of occultism has long out-lived its usefulness – if indeed it ever had any! It seems to us – AC included – that somewhere behind it all, there was a sort of plot or conspiracy. Certain persons had contrived, a long time ago, to inter-twine magic, religion and politics. For some reason best known to themselves, they chose to add on a sort of heavy, Hebrew aspect, about which I have already spoken.[152] In other words, the majority of occultists from pre-Renaissance times onward – were not just 'in error' ... they were powerfully misled.

Whatever the mystic knowledge might have been, a rather dense smoke-screen was put around all. In evidence of this fact, I point out that every single esoteric system speaks of a stage of spiritual development beyond which only semi-mythical persons have been thought to have gone. Here, one thinks of people such as Comte St Germain, Christian Rosenkreutz, and Fulcanelli. The magical bull's-eye is never defined. They don't say much about the more general target either. As a matter of fact, one gets

152. See Chapter 3.

the distinct impression that, although they are enthusiastic and perhaps even sincere, they feel themselves to be at a loss. In teaching others to swim, they themselves get out of their depth at times!

Of course there is a type of personality, usually referred to as 'authoritarian', which makes ideal robots. Once they accept your right to be boss, they will obey your orders, and give their own orders, in an implacable and unquestioning manner. It is this factor which makes excellent Fascists. Such people will shoot their own grand-mothers if told to do so, and they may never have the slightest pangs of conscience. Needless to add that this type of personality is attracted to certain occult 'Orders'.

If their adopted Order happens to allow a central position to the teachings of AC, then they fall into a trap. He made it easy for bigots to take his 'Law of Thelema' and interpret it in several different ways. As happened in the case of Christianity, a large number of schisms and heresies developed, each of which believes it is right. There are many 'sorts' of Golden Dawns, and several versions of the 'O.T.O.'. Each of them believes it alone is right. Each justifes or tries to legitimize its own existence by some contorted appeal to Aleister's teachings.

It hardly matters which of these, if any, is nearest to the mark. Crowley knew better than to revolutionize occultism by revealing his own discoveries too early. I know of Catholic Priests who are 'occultists'. They conceal that fact in order to guide their flock by a less obvious path towards the truth. So there have been, and are still today, 'orthodox occultists' who appear to toe the party-line while working to sink the party. Here I am thinking of the 'Lords of Chaos' with whom these occult orders may have no conscious link.

Number and Zero

Let me stress once again, most occultists have been seduced by the false trail. Naturally, they defend their stance. But unlike normal intelligent people, they seem unable to consider any argument against it. Their minds are as completely closed as, say, those of a Jesuit. "No matter what you say, no matter what proof you offer, I shall not change my mind!" They call this a 'declaration of faith'. It sounds more like brain-washing to me.

Suppose that the Origin of Everything was neither a white-bearded God, nor a big bang! Instead, try to imagine a situation (almost impossible, I agree) where all that existed was total disorder. Then imagine that some 'Gigantic Will' gave the command or took the steps to make 'order' appear. One immense comb would have done the trick. Or one cosmic garden-rake. Out of chaos were born number, regularity, rhythm, pattern and – predictability or future. It is these things alone which may give meaning to the concept of existence. If there is 'being' then it is because there is a pulse, a breathing rate, a brain-wave, light, and the wave-like forms of energy in the cosmos.

The occultist is someone who trains himself to be a 'surfer on the tides of time'. Evil is whatever force or being which seeks to pull down order into chaos and energy into inertia. In his own mundane way, mankind tries to express this fundamental shift as a kind of fall. Angels fell from heaven through pride. Adam and Eve fell from God's grace through disobedience. The living fall, soldiers fall, the Roman Empire fell. We notice that all forms of life react *against* the inertia of matter and gravity. Trees lift their branches, flowers thrust up their flowers, and we humans – we "lift our eyes to the mountains".

On the other hand, we tend to speak of Hell, the home of the Lord of Chaos, as the pit, the infernal (inferior) depths, or the abyss. That is what we fall down to. That is what is waiting for us unless we 'do'. All this is a pale memory of the first knowledge: that you and I have been 'lifted up', out of a sea of chaos. Hence the occult fascination, in the Middle Ages, with architecture, cathedrals, and Pythagoras etc. Hence too, the artificially invented liaison by the Hasidic Jews of the Kabbalah, with its novel use of 'number'. Whatever qualities the people of Israel might possess, it is not this one which is going to raise their status in the world's eyes.

Parallel Realities

AC knew how to span the 'distance' (even though distance is not really involved) between what I call "*this world, here and now*" and "*that world, there and then*". Without doubt, most people will assume that we are referring to the normal, physical world and the astral plane. No, I'm not. *This world, here and now* is our existing reality which appears to our senses to be quite stable. It is the 'laws' of this reality which we accept as 'science'. But *that world there and then* is a quite 'other' reality, where the same rules no longer apply.

It has often been said that magic is a form of primitive science. I put the shoe on the other foot: science is an attempt to explain or understand certain things which may simply be 'beyond our intellectual capacity'. Or, to be more precise, the concepts are beyond our grasp when our brain is functioning in a 'normal' state. That some of us do 'wander across', or 'stray beyond the bounds', is not so much a sign of 'madness' as proof that stares us in the face.

The people concerned with the Montauk Project express their ideas in terms of wave-forms, wavicles, gaps in time, and so on. When we occultists (i.e., occultists of my school) speak of 'this world, here and now', and 'that world, there and then', I believe we are talking about the same things. Our terms are different because, as children, we were pressed into different moulds. Our ways of thinking are different too, because of the various ways in which our intellects were trained. But just as, for example, the O.T.O. might have been misled by Crowley's use of 'things Egyptian' as an extensive metaphor, and not as a reality – so might persons trained as scientists be misled by – the patterns already imprinted on their brains.

After all, if Mr Nichols and those others, did have their minds manipulated, by what means can they be certain that the manipulation is not just going through another phase? I often refer to 'Alice in Wonderland' and 'Alice Through the Looking Glass', and remind people that these delightful stories were written by a professor of mathematics. He encapsulates some of the problems which perplexed him, and here and there he also offers his solutions. One of the 'oddities' is the reversed (but not inverted) image that we see in a mirror.

I have even proposed (as have some writers of horror stories) that the 'mirror world' exists. Just as the two helices of DNA, could not co-exist in a left-handed or right-handed world, so each being throws his own 'shadow' and has a 'counter-existence'. If ever you should meet your own 'double',[153] above all – do not shake hands! It would be like the two halves of a sand-glass swallowing each other.

Normally, there is division or barrier standing between 'this world, here and now' and 'that world, there and then'. In

153. 'Doppleganger' in German, and adopted as the technical term for such a phenomenon.

138

common language, we refer to it as 'death'. But if the barrier exists between two, conflicting states of reality, then that barrier is not necessarily permanent.

'Myself when young did eagerly frequent
Both poet and saint and heard great argument
about it and about, but evermore
Came out by that same door wherein I went.'[154]

Voices from Beyond

In his 'magic' – or in his way of *comprehending things* – the bona fide occultist tries to make contact with 'powers' or 'energies', and to seek out their source, or the Great Will which imposed Order on Chaos. Following all the 'hints' and 'clues' which are scattered through religious and occult literature, AC and I both realized that we come into this world not by spontaneous combustion, but by sex. All you have to do is couple this with Wilhelm Reich's theories of 'orgone', and it bursts on you with a blinding light that – quite apart from being 'nice' – sex might also conceal or contain the very energy by which we could achieve the ultimate truth.

Just as the Mafia seeks exactly the same 'external signs of wealth', that we all strive for ... (though honest citizens use approved means (i.e., work), whereas the Mafia uses outlawed means (i.e., violence)) there is a parallel that we can trace with so-called 'Black Magic'. Its followers, the Black Magicians, want exactly the same access to powers and energies – but are willing to ignore 'The Law' to obtain them. I have said before that mankind is the kind of animal which 'huddles'. We are designed, by descent, to live in herds and in communities. Black magic seeks to destroy these basic rules of our being and lead us toward a state of chaos.

In modern times, their most successful gambit has been to make people mentally and emotionally ill ... and to make use of sexual urges in order to achieve this. Hence my scorn of the basic attitude of the Christian Church. However sincerely duped they may be, they have been the cause of an immense amount of suffering and death.

154. 'Rubaiyat of Omar Khayyam', trans. Edward Fitzgerald (1859).

AC was not a black magician. On several occasions he made contact with 'that world there'. Knowing of the Kaiser's plans, and after him of Hitler's plans, he made a point of deliberately sabotaging their key efforts. One of the true reasons why Hitler was so anti-semitic was that the Jewish religion has 'swallowed' and 'digested' other nearby religions ... including the notion of a 'Monstrous Power', which the Bible refers to as Behemoth.

It is my opinion, and one that I have not reached lightly, that all the 'German' names and connections in occult circles have a significance. You will undoubtedly find that on the opposite side, among those who were resisting the plot, there were a number of Jewish names too. Hubbard was involved because he was, so to speak, an 'occult fascist', and his system of dianetics was a method roughly equivalent to that of the bees. Except that he was collecting 'soul energy'.

I am only too sorry that films like 'Ghostbusters', which was very amusing, have already prepared the ground for ridicule. One might well ask, whose creative imagination dreamed up the stories for such films and books? But we must not automatically dismiss the truth just because Hollywood gave it 'the treatment' first. Cecil B. De Mille had a stab at Moses, twice, much to everyone's distaste. But I doubt if anyone believes in Hollywood as a guiding light.

On the 12th August 1943, AC, myself, and five other people were gathered round an ancient stone monument, called Men-an-Tol, near Morvah in Cornwall, England. You may note the similarity of the name to Montauk, and indeed etymology shows that the two names are linked by the same root meaning. His diary does not mention this visit.[155] Neither does it mention many other things. He did not write it for posterity, you know, but rather for those people whose eyes pried everywhere. He was, as I have already pointed out, a secret agent for several countries! But curiously enough, he did write in his diary: "Fortieth anniversary of my first marriage."

The stone itself is called a 'quoit' because it has a large circular hole in it. I was made to lie on a length of board, and this was inserted (me with it) into the hole. It was like the ferrite rod that

---

155. The signs, marks, ciphers and peculiar numbers to be found in his diaries are something more than a record of his sexual acts. This is how the world reads them, but he stopped putting notches on his gun when he was in his teens.

is put into an electric coil. Aleister performed a ritual which appeared to 'cause' a line of 'rough water' between this spot in southern England, and Long Island in the USA.

On the 12th August 1923, Aleister Crowley was in the desert, just outside of Tunis, where he had been 'on retreat' with Leah Hirsig and Norman Mudd. As a companion, he had an Arab boy called (surprise, surprise!) Mohammed. They were in the tent of an important sheik who acknowledged Crowley as a Master. It was on this occasion that they prepared the way for Crowley to become the new head of the Karl Germer branch of the O.T.O.

On the 12th August 1903, Crowley married Rose Kelly. But during the consummation of their nuptuals, he not only had a serial orgasm, but also a vision to do with the 'The Book of Desolation'. Since the latter deals, among other things, with the "wiles of chaos", I can see a clear link. He was directed to go to Paris and to search in, on, or near the tomb of the same Hoehné Wronski, to whom I've already referred.

Things begin to hang together, don't they?

21

TEZCATLIPOCA

In Aztec, "Smoking Mirror": the God of Warriors and Avenger of misdeeds

Disease of all Types

I don't know if you've ever noticed just how often, in films or books, a psychiatrist is represented as being round the twist himself? Have you ever remarked how society is prepared to tolerate behaviour, which it would normally condemn, if it is shown by some very gifted or talented personality? You must tack on to this one further idea – the fact that it is we, the people who make up a society, who define what 'madness' is. Then, I think, you can perhaps see why we say that 'genius is next to madness'.

There is a type of 'divine madness' which grips great actors, musicians, and performers of all types. I have described 'ecstasy'[156] as being quite similar to temporary schizophrenia. I have described sexual orgasm as "a state of physical, emotional and mental exaltation in which one's soul undergoes convulsions". Not to waste time nor mince my words, it is only when a 'human sheep' decides to 'change' that he re-opens natural, ancient, pathways of communication across Mr Nichols' 'grid'.

One member of the Montauk Research Group, Mr Al Bielek, used massive computer power to arrive at the conclusion that the noxious and dangerous effects of those early experiments were part of a 'UFO Conspiracy'. In one way, this shows great imagination, because it matches one set of 'unknown' factors with

156. From the Greek, *ex histemi*, which means: someone put out of his place.

another set. But I'm afraid that the imaginative powers did not go far enough. I think that Mr Bielek was side-tracked.

First of all, any communications that were received might well have been 'lifted' out of one's own fantasies and 'tailored' into a shape and form that you are almost eager to buy.

Second, bearing in mind that we are studying the space-time continuum – then it doesn't much matter who or what is trying to communicate with us. It is just as likely to be on the same space wave but at a different time. I have mentioned that I am what is often called a 'medium', and that I am capable of being 'taken over' by 'spirits'. What I did not explain was that these intelligences or entities might not always be from the past – but from our own future ... that is to say: their own, current reality.

All the other phenomena that one associates with this type of spiritist phenomenon – temperature change, sudden breezes, objects moving etc. – it could all be a physical *epiphenomenon*. It has no great significance as regards the main, or central purpose but is just a sort of side-effect or by-product. However much one might be tempted, one should read nothing into it except that they support the idea of disturbances in the space-time continuum. If it is lightning which causes thunder, is the thunder itself of any importance at all? No! It can be accepted as a kind of witness to events.

Doesn't this make sense of all those trumpets, rose petals and other 'apports' which cause the sceptic to smile? Doesn't this explanation take in all the rest ... music, voices, chains, hoots, and phosphorescence? Hauntings and ghosts hardly ever react to 'this reality', i.e., the one in which they appear to us. They are probably a replay of a 'far off reality' which has been triggered by someone's powerful emotions. What is different, and much rarer, is when one of these spirits reacts to us and seems aware of our proximity.

What couldn't a hostile nation achieve, if it could make a nuclear blast 'replay' as and when it wished – or if it could have ghosts carry weapons from one dimension to another? Come to that, why not oblige them to bring a virus from their reality to this one, e.g., the one which causes AIDS? It is not at all common to witness a new disease in development. It very rarely happens. Yet everyone seems to accept the facts if and when they do appear.

Nobody thinks too much about how those facts were brought about.

But isn't there a strange and almost overpowering synchronicity between (a) the growing tolerance of homosexuality, and (b) the use of homosexual contact as a vector for the spread of AIDS? No, no, no! I am certainly not hinting at any sort of divine punishment. I am thinking of a military diversion tactic that has taken our attention away from something more insidious still: the virus is in the process of changing and it is attacking the heterosexual population too.

Is this how the world shall end? Not with a bang, but a whimper? Shall the 'Day of Judgement' be one last rustle of bandages, and then silence?

Inner Powers

Have you ever noticed that some people, when you meet them for the very first time, seem to take energy out of you? They don't know that they are doing it, of course. They may derive some benefit or advantage. They may feel better at the end of the day. But I do not believe that they are yet conscious of what they are about.

Perhaps they are a sort of 'astral vampire[157]'? For my own part, I do believe that the myths and legends about vampires have come down to us from very ancient times. They pre-date the celebrated Vlad Dracul by several thousand years. This means that if Dracula did exist, then he was not the first.

Now suppose that the 'energy' they stole was not in the form of blood, nor yet even of sperm[158] – but was composed of negative emotion or, as Mr Nichols' puts it, "Dead Orgone" or "DOR"? Now if we may be candid, in the interest of furthering our knowledge, this 'physical' sexual seduction is only going to rob a person of either semen or vaginal juices. Since we can churn these out by the bucketful, we cannot assume that they are either rare or precious. But when the energy (or orgone) is invoked,[159] all the

157. See Chapter 16.
158. As is suggested by the legend of Incubi and Succubi – demonic entities that specialize in sexually debauching young people in their sleep.
159. This energy is not 'produced' or 'created' by the human body. Whatever it is that one does in order to achieve sexual climax, this can also attract energy (or orgone) from 'out there'. It is when this positive power meets our own negative emotions that there is a sort of 'explosion' of matter and anti-matter, as it were.

144

powers of the space-time dimension are at our disposal – momentarily! Perhaps now you can see why sex drives some people mad and leads others to a state of sublime detachment.

But this explains why certain people do provoke sadness and heaviness of spirit. It is almost as if they fed on grief and despair. There are certain people you may even take as sexual partners, and from that moment on your physical and spiritual health begins to go downhill. I accept that all this is extremely difficult to swallow, and yet it is an adequate explanation for the larger part of these phenomena. If you had worked as long as I have in the field of mental illness, you would be far less sceptical. I wasn't the only one. There are thousands of qualified psychiatric nurses to whom you might speak. Failing all else, have a look at the film called 'Mr Frost'.[160] When I add up all the experiences I have had, I don't feel that it would be an exaggeration to announce that "They are among us now!"

But if such forces are truly tied up with sexuality in some way, then one can see the significance perhaps of 'pointed stakes' and 'hammers'. The difficult one to pin down, is the 'garlic'. To understand what part it might play, we have to go back to the pharaonic times and study the way that they turned corpses into mummies. Above all, one must recollect their reasons for doing so. They believed that 'another time' would come.

I have often pointed to the frequency of German names among occult circles. It may be a coincidence and yet I don't think so. What we have to remember is that the O.T.O., the Golden Dawn, and the Rosicrucians were all founded in Germany ... and all connected with German, Protestant Freemasonry. We must also bear in mind the historical facts that Germany, or its predecessor Prussia, has been a cause of war and conquest for centuries. From the Teutonic Knights onward, the philosophy of Fascism has been pushing its head through the ground.

When you think of "Superman", "Pure Being", and "Might is Right", don't you also think of Nietzsche, Schopenhauer, and that team? The O.T.O. was 'used' by the English and the American secret services in both world wars. They won't admit it – they may not even be aware of it – but their membership is still infiltrated at quite a high level. Now only yesterday, as I write these words,

160. I don't want to give away the plot, but keep your eyes peeled for who has the last smile.

I told a guest that she was pregnant. Much as she would welcome the news, she said it was impossible. She had been 'on the pill' and had had her last period only twenty-five days before. But she rushed to buy a test-kit, and I was right. How did I know? I felt the presence. That is how I detect secret agents too. I can 'feel' their presence.

Four Horsemen of the Apocalypse

This is why Aleister was persuaded to write material favourable to Germany during the First World War. He really did do it at the behest of the secret service. They also wanted him to nominate a certain person to be head of the O.T.O. in America.

One of the more macabre and intriguing things to do with the Montauk Project, is the question concerning the body of a scientist called Nikolas Tesla. He died in 1943, the same year of the Philadelphia Experiment. But the rumour has always been that someone else was either killed in his place, or some convenient corpse was substituted for his, and that he was whisked away to Europe. Neither of these rumours is true.

I have it from Aleister Crowley that Nikolas Tesla was killed and that his brain was removed. As a scientist he had been getting rebellious about the dangerous risks that the US government was prepared to take – or if not the government, then Dr von Neumann. Since he was a man of high standing and of scholarly repute, the problem was how to remove him as an obstacle ... and yet keep his intelligence? That is why they took his brain.

Now the techniques of cryogenics were not then available. They just didn't know how to freeze the brain in liquid nitrogen. They had to resort to ice. They slowly froze the living Tesla, and replaced the cerebro-spinal fluid with physiological saline at a very low temperature. When he died, the brain tissues did not suddenly expand (with ice) and so disintegrate. The specimen was brought to Europe where it still exists, although advanced modern techniques are being applied to it.

Nikolas Tesla was born in 1856 in what is now Croatia. He was, therefore, nineteen years older than Aleister Crowley. The strange thing is that Tesla knew Gregori Rasputin, and through him he met Aleister Crowley. All three of them got to know Wilhelm Reich. They did not meet all that frequently, and when meetings took place, they did not last for very long. The contact was conducted by other means – and I don't mean letters. Tesla was an impressive psychic.

It is interesting too to remark the similarity between their ideas vis-à-vis sexuality. All of them held that the sexual energy, no matter what name you give it, would also have a *sinusoidal form*. Tesla was all for pinning it down in Ansgtrom Units, Reich wanted to "collect and condense" it, Rasputin wanted to use it for its potential healing capacity, and Aleister wanted it to work magic. I am more interested in its source and the reasons for its existence.

Each of the four men developed his own method for accessing this energy and for applying it in this 'reality'. I don't think it matters very much what one chooses to call it, so let's not get trapped into an argument about terms. How much further forward would that get us?

One of the purposes of this energy (orgone, or that which lies behind the sexual urge) appears to have been: the ability to shift the conscious mind from 'this time' to 'that time'. In other terms, what psychologists often refer to as 'atavistic dreams' are nothing less than temporary shifts to another reality. Poor old Wilhelm Reich was something of an embarrassment for the US government. They weren't quite sure what he was on about, but in an era when Hollywood love-making involved keeping one foot on the floor ... Reich's ideas about orgone made everyone gulp.

There were also things that Reich did not say. For example, the French have a way of referring to orgasm as "the little death". It might be slightly more precise to translate it as "a slight dying", because there is a certain mystic reverence for love in France. Now let us juxtapose a statement from the Holy Bible: "... greater love hath no man than that he lay down his life for his friends." Gradually, very gradually, we begin to discern a meaning in those coded, enigmatic statements from this ancient book: Leviathan, Behemoth, and the Beast with Seven Heads and Seven Crowns etc.

That said, is it not time to revise all our opinions about spirit seances, telepathy, clairvoyance, and every type of 'mystic' phenomenon?

22

WAKAN TANKA KI

The great and universal God of Sioux Indians

What is Occult?

Occultism is a bundle of things, most of which go back thousands of years. It embraces several ideas at once, which is why it's so hard to spell out. Another problem is that people tend to inspect it, rather than sample it. 'What's it for?' they ask. Even if they don't know, they go straight ahead and use it. On the other hand, it is close to being a religion, since it deals with the sacred and unknown.

Most people like to dabble provided they do not get 'heavily involved'. But what does that mean? Mostly it is when the costs get too high, or when it takes up too much time. Young folk are not as earnest as they claim. As with 'marriage', they like it brief, not lasting. Their span of enthusiasm is that of a cigarette. Their faith is 'now' and 'me'. They think they are excited and sincere, but the Gods know them too well. They do not get very far, though they give it all they've got ... until the next craze. Take the 'Hare Krishna' thing. How many are over fifty?

We need several signposts to pinpoint 'The Occult'.

> 1. It is a Belief to do with life, death, and truth.
> 2. It is a Door which opens hidden energies.
> 3. It is a Way of thought which transcends Self Will.
> 4. It is a Bridge that joins one with 'all'.
> 5. It is a Temple for our true nature.
> 6. It is a Mountain whence one glimpses the Gods.
> 7. It is a Light that blinds the lie.

148

The majority of 'experts' prefer not to explain. They have a strange passion for adding more and more mystery. It could be that they don't want you to know. It could also be that they don't know much themselves. In each case, you can guess what they would say.

In the way the western mind operates, magic seems to be the helpful aspect of the theories taught by an occult teacher. But to be quite precise, it actually means the ability to handle and control our reality 'now' via a system of symbols.

An alphabet, or some other system of making marks to portray speech, is a system of symbols. The same is true of musical notation and also the way that chemists can write down formulae. Road signs are just one more system, and so are algebra, poetry, ballet and hallowed ritual. To a certain extent then, a worker in these skills is just someone who has the ability to handle the symbols. He can put his sense into other systems of logic, and move one 'reality' into 'another'.

In a sense, this is rather like Caesar or Napoleon planning a battle, on a desktop, by using maps and model soldiers! But later on, they can transfer the 'meaning' from the desktop onto a field of battle. This is where Hitler went wrong and where Churchill foiled him. You too could go wrong if you don't respect your correct place in the general scheme of things.

It is one thing to dole out sonorous titles, such as 'Adeptus Templi', as a prize for learning material by rote memory. It is quite another thing actually to change reality – and keep one's mental sanity. At the end of the day, there is a sense in which we are the magic in which we think we are merely involved. Whatever we may do, or may not do, is a process by which we fashion our own destiny.

Old Ideas

You are not *what you think you are*, but *what you think*. The thoughts in your mind affect your body, your health, your behaviour and your soul. This is clearest in the sexual aspect of life. Very few people realize that they are dealing with a source of magical power.[161] It was bad when 'morality' made these urges taboo. It is worse still when we stomp over the limits of nature.

161. We invoke the 'male force' or the 'female force' so casually, and we so often leave them frustrated. We create, if you like, our personal 'ley-lines' which then go on to make things worse.

149

'Freedom' is a murky concept. It means one thing to the man in prison, another to the anarchist, and something else to the poor wretch stricken with cancer. In fact, 'freedom' does not have a fixed meaning. When you use the word, you should specify what you mean. As a matter of fact, what it means depends on your motive[162] as you speak. To put it bluntly – 'freedom' is in your head.

Magic is like that too. My grandma thought that TV was magic. Her grandma would have been awe-struck by a bus. In a way, magic is whatever stumps your mind. If it is easily done, or if you know how it's done, then it's less likely to be magic. Magic is what lies beyond daily life and outside normal reality.[163] You are the standard against which you measure magic. Therefore, you are the obstruction that causes magic to fail. I am not speaking about hypnosis, or auto-suggestion. I am telling you that magic is an aspect of Will. Man is the only creature to have it.

This is why we need not fear 'Black Magic'. If a person has such basic flaws that only evil attracts him, then it stands to reason that our power is greater. If we had defects, we mended them ourselves. We have already become the Masters of our own being. They are the Slaves of What Rules them.

A stupid concept is not improved by being 'ancient'. A good concept is not to be dismissed just because it is 'new'. Our own life is short. We would like it to be longer. Hence we have an in-built reverence for antiquity and age. But the Gods who permit the advance of learning are 'outside of time'. They do not mean to dazzle us. They know we are capable of 'perceiving differently'.

It is harmful to be proud of our technical progress. It is the wrong emphasis and we detract from the status of Gods. How little we know when compared with how great are our fears. And yet, both wisdom and fear have their origin inside 'self', and that 'self' is just illusory. We must learn to see from outside. We must try the asylum door and learn it was never locked.

We are filled with such wonder at what we see, we do not quite realize that we too are being observed. If the 'Watcher' were on this dimension then, surely, we would have known? If it is on

162. The same thing applies to the two words 'masculine' and 'feminine', and what they mean does differ from one culture to another.
163. If you have never travelled widely, then a faraway place can seem magical. But what I mean here is: that side of natural life which we neglect.

some other plane, then how may we make contact? We only recently found out that our body was made up of cells. That helped us to look for 'rogue cells' and so treat cancer. But there are other things, smaller still, whose existence we can only infer. Now if we cannot chat to a virus, how dare we hope to address the Gods? How can we pass the boundary which separates physical from mystical?

Martyrs

Magic means changing one's views, checking one's opinions, and taking a closer look at our received wisdom. It might all be so stale that it is indigestible. Not to mince words, there is a lot we must 'un-know' before we can 'know anew'. But so much stale bread is about. Almost every young person has nibbled some. This is why they expect that Gods and Religion are matters of popular vote – that the golden secret is 'democracy'.

"We've elected a new God," they scream.

"Let's hope the old one is willing to step down," I reply.

"We go where we fucking want," they spit.

"Then tell Him where so that He can join you," I explain.

As a Teacher employed by the Gods, the toughest nut to crack is men's faulty logic. They are used to being *told* what to think and they don't know *how* to do it. They are like the rats a laboratory has trained to run through mazes. Open the cage and they wouldn't know what else to do. They have been trapped inside a dream. Ninety per cent of students don't know who they are. They look at the tag round their neck and read out what it says.

You have your smart-ass students and your timid students. But by far the most common are ones who just want to check me out. The big test is: how far do my ideas agree with theirs? They can only take in ideas they already agree with.

A wiser person might ask: what makes magic work? That must even pass through the mind of an expert from time to time. But an expert can push it out again. There are some thoughts that they dare not probe. Like the shadow in the wardrobe, they won't leave their bed to look. When we were children and first heard certain stories, we weren't at all curious. 'Open Sesame' would roll back the rock of Ali-Baba's cave. We never asked how it was done. It was taken at face value. In our 'childhood reality', it's the sort of thing that rocks did.

We never questioned it then, and we don't question it now. So if a book tells you to do 'A Lesser Banishing Ritual', you do it. Have you banished anything? Was there anything there to be banished? Did the magic work? If it failed, would you ever know? Your philosophy is a bit like leaving a note for the milkman. The bloody bottles come, don't they? This is cookbook magic. You just collect the recipes. But what about the 'gas', the 'electricity' or 'energy'? Or will the ingredients just cook themselves?

No. You must rustle up some power. You must know how to control it because, like gas or electricity, it can kill. And do not summon demons the way you hail a taxi! Indeed, don't summon a single, sodding thing until you know what the cost will be. After all, even Rambo would back off if you opened the sluice-gates of hell. Rambo more than others!

Mythical Books[164] don't help. Nor does The Key of Solomon. As for sacred texts – the Bible, the Koran, or the Tripitaka – none of them is what it claims to be. I'm sorry if this offends you. But you should not believe what you've seen at the cinema. Why should a piece of printing 'work'? Would 'Holy Water' work for a Jew? Would gestures from Memphis work on spirits from Tibet? Would the pretty Celtic crystals protect you from African fiends? Let's be blunt, shall we? Why should anything in '*this world*' have the slightest effect in '*that world*'?

I have seen people die from a touching faith in their own fictions. You may be nice people. Your hearts may glow with light and honesty. But are you any better equipped than the Christians who went to face the lions? The church calls them 'Martyrs'. I call it 'suicide'. The lions most likely called them 'sitting ducks'.

Training

We can switch off one kind of conduct, (e.g., being a butcher), and switch on another, (e.g., being the life and soul of a party). We are quite adept at playing as a drunk, peeling off, or doing erotic things with pickled onions. We have tiny psychic photos: 'me at a party', 'me in church', and 'me up the creek'. This is why we know what to do in most ordinary situations. But we don't often meet spirits. We have rarely stood at the gates of eternity.

164. e.g., the 'Necronomicon'.

We have never before been visited by a God. When these things happen for the first time, don't ring 999.

One needs to adapt to circumstances. The best gimmick is, rip your mask off, and show your true self. That's not easy when most of your life you've been taught to pretend. The most worrying part of all is that you don't know if or when you've succeeded. By the same token, neither do you know if you've failed. When you come face to face with magic, you are loitering in the same zone which some experts would label madness. Hence the need for training. One of these days you may need to find your way back.

The way of magic is too simple. Oh yes, I'm afraid so. Either that or our minds are too complex. We approach the Occult with such unworthy hopes. So widespread is this, I tell my own students that *they* are their own worst enemy. At all events, those who would be articled[165] need to find a Master who is willing to take them on. But at this point, two more snags arise. First, Masters are not all that thick on the ground. Second, very few persons can accept the rules that go with being a student.

As quick as possible, a student has to change his goals and stop asking for personal benefit or gain. He must think in terms of his private ordeals and how best to enhance '*The Great Work*'. In short, his vision must expand, move outward, and take in others, the world, the universe. This is not all that easy when your horizons have been limited to local suburbs, the cinema or the nearby shopping centre. And a master does not expect one to abandon the path through fatigue, modesty, fear or lack of time. One person commits himself for every twenty who want to taste the lollipop.

It is quite likely that we are the only form of life in the cosmos. We must not be clouded by maths or by chance. The critical items for the growth of sentient life were at a precise distance from the centre of the big bang.[166] I'm sorry to spoil the fun, but mankind is not a 'flock' of experimental animals put here a million years ago by UFOs. The truth is more awesome, and less like a nursery rhyme. It is our destiny to spread our seed across the Milky Way.

165. Bound by a legal contract.
166. cf. 'Cosmic Coincidence', Gribbin and Reese, Black Swan 1991.

We know our own planet. There was no sign of urbanism before a certain date. Out of their limited factual knowledge, gleaned mainly from 'colour supplements', people come up with theories that match their own dreams. But I repeat the same warning over and over again: *the past means less than we think.* Each memory, whether it be racial, tribal or personal, is meant to bring more wisdom for tomorrow. We are here to help the onward progress of the Plan and not to collect old bottles. The start is, and was, always now. Time is just one of those mental confines that we allow to confuse us.

You want to work magic? Then you must find a way to tackle some concepts which lie beyond the capacity of your brain. You must be able to turn an 'image' into 'reality'.

It is not a proviso that you believe in 'God' before you can study the occult. Nor is it asked that you can already work magic before signing up as a student. But rather like an aspirant for a Drama School, you must first display some sign of talents. Having made that analogy, I should explain that Drama has its origins in magic, and that many students would benefit from training methods used in certain drama schools.

What we are both seeking is a trait we call 'the touch'. As usual, this is not at all precise. Over the decades we have grown a bit careless or else the letters do not signify what they used to. What I should say is that we are seeking a mark which shows the Gods have touched you.

If you lack this mark then, together, we must arrange to inspire them to give it you.

23
BORVO

The Gallic God of magic springs and bubbling hearts

Royal Bones

The mood was different during the War years. For a while, Britain was the only country in Europe not under the heel of the Nazi jack-boot! She stood alone as, after more than a thousand years, the Huns were on the rampage again. The Occult is still a power to reckon with in Germany. But the two World Wars saw a vast change in the monarchic systems. Each of these states forsook the magic energy of royalty:

Albania	Afghanistan	Austria	Bulgaria	Burma
China	Egypt	Ethiopia	Germany	Greece
Hungary	India	Iraq	Iran	Italy
Libya	Malaya	Manchuria	Pakistan	Portugal
Syria	Rumania	Russia	Turkey	Tunis
Yemen	Yugoslavia...	etc.		

There was great respect for the monarchy and those hollow words, "For King and Country", still aroused the spirit. Nobody would have been hostile if the allies had revived the Hapsburg Empire. If the plan had won through then Central and Eastern Europe would have been safe from the Red Flag of Communism. The world economy would have been a very different thing.

This is hard to see when events are so remote. The actors are just sepia ghosts in silent films. Was Rasputin a real man? Did Hitler truly exist? We are not as shocked as people were then. The news is no longer new. The human heart cannot stay enraged for ever. This is why you may have missed a strange event.

About the time my first book appeared, the KGB issued a press release via the Russian Embassy in Paris.[167] They stated that they had prior knowledge of the Hess Affair even though Churchill and Roosevelt had kept it secret from their wartime allies! What an odd thing to say! What an odd time to say it! No-one saw the connection with my work!

I don't know if you have noticed, but the Masons have begun to take an interest in Public Relations. They are taking one or two steps to improve their public image. Of course, you don't do this unless it were necessary. As things turned out, it has been a total flop. Have you ever read any of their books? Did you manage to get along to their display? They manage to conceal their *joie de vivre* quite well, don't you think? As a matter of fact, rather like the churches, they are also living in a different century. I wouldn't be surprised if they weren't a bit short of new members too.

A point in passing: Fleet Street is against Prince Charles because he has always refused to join the Masons. The steady campaign to chip at his status is an attempt to force his hand. They want a King they can control, or they'll change things like they did in America and France!

If you'd like to be invited to join Masonry, you had better get ready. You could begin by learning the scheme of secret gestures which is based, loosely, on the Royal Navy Semaphore System. In dire straits you can add urgency to your message by rolling up your trouser-leg. As regards what happened before trousers came into mode – we'd rather you did not ask. But they all repeat the signs and gestures for hours on end. They must get them right to earn an upgrade. In Westminster, they have to transmit twenty verses of 'Eskimo Nell'[168] across the Thames! If you notice anything odd by Cleopatra's Needle, it might be a 'politico' trying to climb higher. Do not call an ambulance or summon the police.

Now whenever I think of horror my mind leaps to what is jokingly called 'the fair sex' and to my own, choice editress. I know. I mention her quite regularly, which is so boring for you all. But she, and her friend, are always in my thoughts. I want them to know that. I hope with all sincerity that they are alive and well, and that life is bringing them all the openings that they both

167. See 'The Times', for 10th June, 1991.
168. Just in case you didn't know: 'Eskimo Nell' is the eponymous heroine of a filthy poem which gets longer and longer as the years go by.

deserve. I think of them each time that Hallowe'en comes round, and I always send them topical regards.

"Ha-ha!" said AC. "Vehemence is the other face of rage, and rage is hate that never forgives!" He did not use the word 'anger'. No-one in his right mind ever does. It comes from Old Norse, you see, and means 'grief' or "you'll be sorry".

It could have been something like this he had in mind when he said: "Priests, princes and odd sods in politics are handy if low spirits are around." In my own case though, things work otherwise. I mean that priests, princes and odd sods in politics make me sad and blue. As you may have noticed, I do not have a very forgiving nature. When I am hurt, or someone tries to offend me, I make a bee-line for '*Lex Talionis*'.[169] I look for redress with all my force!

Okay! It's a fault. But I can't help it. I just do my worst and think about it afterward. No, keep calm. I would not do that with men who publish books or with authors who are honest. But I would do it to those who put pressure on others. "If you are afraid of justice," said Dracula, "always sleep with your eyes open."

Hurtful Things

Speaking of gentlemen's toilets, I have to tell you that my guard-dogs do not like people asking me the time. They don't take kindly to persons who are seeking the last match in London. It's not that I secretly want these persons to suffer invisible or astral attacks but, you do understand, I dare not give a welcoming smile.

In any case, my 'animals' are independent operators – which means they do what they want, when they want. Can you imagine what they'd be capable of if I actually gave them an order? You've seen the aftermath of a hurricane, I dare say – well, my dogs are worse. It's like a tidal wave, the seasonal sales, a football riot and a troop of irate buffalo – all combined. I've had offers from the Serbs! The P.L.O. have been to have a look at them. There was a discreet call from someone who lives at the end of The Mall!

At the moment, I am trying not to let them see my vexation with one or two bookshops. I am not talking about those national chains which deal mainly with magazines and envelopes anyway.

---

169. Most people would know this as: "an eye for an eye and a tooth for a tooth."

Neither do I mean those smaller shops which have no space to stock everything in print, but will gladly take orders. No, I refer to the shops which deal in 'occultism' but which utilise an informal gag. Up in the North, a student asked if they stocked my books. "No, we don't," replied the manager, "we've heard some funny things about him"!

I've heard some even funnier things about them! What's more, all of it came from their own lips! It wasn't all that long ago that they sent round a circular asking for support on a very unsavoury subject. I gave it to them. I got one of my students to send them a cheque. So come on, you guys! Are you looking for a quarrel that would re-open old wounds?

Dafter still was a bookshop in London. A student wanted to buy TEN copies of my second book. The salesman replied: "We don't stock it because there is no demand"! Could his ears hear what his mouth said? Is it someone who is just very bad at maths? Or is it someone who wishes me ill? In either case, I am in a generous mood and I am quite willing to give free lessons. I feel, for the good of his soul, that he must be called to account. So, if he does not deal *fairly* by me, he may end up with a barrow in Berwick Street. Or face the prospect of a tarot card coming alive.

Mind you, I've been given the cold shoulder by better people than him. I would have you know that Her Majesty, the Queen, has ignored me for years. So has the Heir Presumptuous, and every other member of the Royal family. How different it would have been in Queen Victoria's day! She had a great interest in the other world, did that old lady. You can bet your tiara that someone would have noticed how accurate some of my warnings had been. I would have been invited round to tea.

Letters from High
The fact that they don't believe in me doesn't stop them writing. Each sect or cult sniffs through all books to discover anything they find offensive. The next day the author receives a ton of hate-mail. The worst, in order of descent, are devotees of gentle Christ, Jews, the Shiite Muslims, Gay Lib, and the Republic of Ireland. Other writers and I, we have compared notes, and the hate-mail is identical. We have now traced most of them to their source and are sending a message of our own.

A standard letter will express pity for my deformed brain, plus the kindly advice that God, one of His ardent henchmen, or the next speeding Taxi will mow me down. Another suggests that the AIDS virus is one of God's great creations and that it can be targeted at anyone who deserves it. There are the same sort of threats or hints about your portfolio, bank account, family, and even the pet dog. But I don't feel uneasy at all. I have my guards. More than that, AC prepared for my coming. "Your conception," he claimed, "was as immaculate as could be, given that your mother was sea-sick, and it took place in Boulogne!"

Stephen Knight died of a brain tumour a short time after writing his book about the Masons.[170] In their elation, there developed the myth that the Masons had killed him by magical means.[171] This is quite absurd. The Masons are incapable of magic. They can hang Italian bankers from London Bridge or push people under trains. They no doubt have an office that plans little accidents. In Paris, for example, they like a leaking gas-main.

I often get letters which are meant for others. A Gay Lib poster for the Pope, for example, or 'Stop Killing Whales' for the Dalai Lama. I'd have thought it quite easy to tell us apart! I can see the amusing side, but a thought keeps nagging me – *are these other people getting letters meant for me?*

I think I'm being mistaken for some other person. I don't know who it could be. I get asked to launch ships, unveil Memorial Plaques, and open Jumble Sales. There have even been a few proposals of marriage – some of them from women. But how can I be sure that anything was meant for me? Might they not be intended for one of the other world figures? Just to play safe, I pass them on to the Swiss Embassy. They believe that 'Hamlet' is a comedy, so they'll know what to do with them.

Rich and Blind

Why do most people still believe in the soul? The answer is: for comfort. The world is not an easy place to live in. There are barbarian hordes with skis in winter. There are the tourist herds who maraud south in summer. There are the motorways where you can play the game of 'Lemmings', and there are hospitals

170. Stephen Knight, 'The Brotherhood', Granada Publishing, 1983.
171. cf. 'Inside the Brotherhood' by Martin Short, Grafton Books 1989.

where blood is almost as dangerous as water. And if that is not enough, there is always Disneyland. The only way of staying sane is to believe in the prospect of life after the EEC.

In former times, most human beings were treated like cattle. They were hunted, tortured, sent to war, killed and raped, but not necessarily in that order. When you come to think about it, the world hasn't changed much.

The rich live by a different calendar to the rest of us. In place of spring, summer, autumn and winter, they go by the Royal Academy, Henley Regatta, Ascot and grouse shooting. There is a dead part of the year when everyone goes to hide in the country. Then there is 'the season'. If you want to count, you display your children with as much of a splash as possible. There is no need to measure the moon's position in the sky. You know the mating season has opened when they start going to parties again.

But the rich are no longer filthy rich. Country houses are being turned into theme parks. Paintings are being sold off to pay for heating. But what the hell! Dowagers dressed in triple chins still quiz the 'nice young men' for the 'gel'. One goes for money or for title – if possible for both. "Oh mummy," squeals one of the fillies, "Do please buy me that one!" It is a market for breeding stock and they all know it. It keeps social power where it belongs, in the hands of the *ancien regime*.

Strange things can pass via the blood – bleeding is the obvious one, but there's also Mad Cow Disease, and now AIDS. This mongrel nobility is so fond of the family tree – with its whores, its traitors, and its regular pink frill. The top families get caviar from Harrods and cocaine from a man round the corner. The more they inbreed, the higher the risk to their babies. Blue blood is weaker than most and immune to nothing.

It is all so weird when one recalls that Kings were first installed as offerings to the Gods. They were the magic mulch that one sprinkled on the crops.[172] A mashed-up King was very good for drought, blight, floods or bad luck! In the EEC today, farmers wonder if we shouldn't put the clock back. Ritual murder at the Summer Solstice would give a fillip to the tourist trade. There would be even bigger crowds than for Pavarotti and Michael Jackson joined together – which shows how far our standards have fallen.

172. Sir Gordon Fraser 'The Golden Bough', MacMillan 1922.

It's not as though Kings do much any more. If I were King, I'd make it illegal to be a Mason. But then, if I were a mid-wife, I'd exchange them for ferrets at birth. If I were God, ah-ha – if I were God I'd assemble the seven circles of heaven[173] and pose the following question: in which country do the happiest people live? Better still, I'd ask: In which country are people truly free? That would make them scratch their heads!

Isn't it a common human quality always to knock a winner? My own pet target is Sebastian Coe. He is slim, good looking, and can run. I detest him right to his back teeth. Much to my wonder and pride, there are people who actually feel like that about me. Though I'm not a runner. I am more of your roller.

No one can agree on what a Master is. Not being members of the club, they are green with animus. But most folk of an occult turn agree that AC was 'chosen'. He was set up by the Gods. His duty was to guide mankind back to the proper path. I am his son and his successor. If that makes you sick then kindly have the courage to sign up with the enemies. Don't be one of those bizarre persons who does nothing but air opinions for the whole of his life. Be a bit of a devil, and take me on!

As for you younger ones who claim to be followers of Crowley, you sneaked in by the back door. This is why your luck is so lousy. Stop seeing me as if I were 'Typhoid Mary'.[174] You need a Teacher to mend that hole in your head!

173. This is the celestial hierarchy as given by Pseudo-Dionysius.
174. The first 'carrier' to be identified. She could infect anyone with typhoid but showed no symptoms of the disease herself.

24

ADRASTE

The Goddess of War in ancient Britain[175]

Hook, Line and Sinker

AC had a strange sense of humour. When he did or said anything funny, it was mainly to amuse himself. He wasn't trying to make an audience applaud. He never said or did anything but that there were other levels of meaning. If he made you laugh, then you could be sure there was an important point being made. If he said something grave, then you could also be sure that he was playing with you too. How can I describe it? Like a tangled film, written by Harold Pinter, acted by Monty Python, and directed by Fritz Lang. One hardly dared to chuckle in case one missed something.

Even in dying, I'm not sure it wasn't a joke. I smile now, as I smiled then, with my mouth corners turning down with disquiet in case I mistook him. But I did not mourn. No, I did not mourn. I wished him 'bon voyage' and, from that moment on, kept eyes and ears open for fleeting glimpses or muffled whispers from the astral plane. That would have meant that either Crowley was keeping in touch … or that other occupants were moving out!

As regards AC's message, I am more worried about the young folk who wolf things down without so much as chewing them. I don't think they even know what the word 'insight' means. But it is not at all good for the soul to swallow things hastily. It is possible that they feel themselves to be in the presence of an older man who is Holy and therefore safe. But the world is run by older men. There are not all that many teenage dictators or army chiefs with acne still. Nevertheless, there are a few!

175. When Queen Boudicca captured Roman women, she had them sacrificed to this goddess, whose name meant 'invincible one'.

One thing they will learn as they get older is that age in itself does not necessarily bring wisdom. "There is no fool like an old fool," Aleister used to say. I wish that young people would learn this. I wish they would also realize that even when one is wise, it is quite possible for one to be wrong. AC was superb in the role of Aleister Crowley, but I noticed that his costume was not 'whiter than white'. He had his flaws. He had his weak points. Which of us has not? The problem is more fundamental than this, for when someone is a Master, it means that the Beyond has licensed him to guide and teach. But have we any right to expect him to be perfect?

In Crowley's own case, he was not at all well equipped to be a world teacher. He was much better adapted to a small, élite coterie. To put it bluntly, I was only the second poor person who ever came into his life. The first was my mother.

Things are made far worse when we realize that (a) Crowley wrote books mainly because he needed money, and (b) he rarely revealed what he actually knew. This doesn't stop the impetuous young ones from getting the truth the wrong way round. I've heard them: beardless gurus sitting in a Lotus posture on a rolled-up sleeping bag. They shine with honesty, no doubt about it, but that in no way alters the fact that they are wrong. Hitler was sincere, I am sure, but it was no comfort to any of his victims.

But for those who are zealous, pure emotion can alter lies into truth. "I believe," they say. "I feel it in my guts. So it must be true." On this basis, one could make a similar claim for blocked bowels, diarrhoea or orgasm. No, I'm sorry, they have no vocation. What they are hearing is just the call of nature![176]

Graphology

I went to a seminar once on new insights into mental tests. That evening, in the bar, one of the other members, an American as it happens, started to preach the value of graphology.[177] Before you could say 'Carl Rogers', they all dropped their air of neutral observers and began shoving notes or envelopes under his nose.

176. When I was a child, this was a very polite way of saying you needed to use the toilet. It may still be in use, but in England and France I am often startled when people say "I've got to have a piss" or "I'm going for a shit". This new candour can be dire for those with a powerful sense of imagery.
177. Reading character by analysis of a person's hand-writing.

These bits of paper were all anonymous. He asked that everyone use a pseudonym, such as Mickey Mouse or Jules Verne.

Of course, there is a lot of significance to be read into the false names that people choose.[178] But that's another story. This fellow then picked up pieces of paper at random and gave a description of the writer's character and physical appearance. There were gasps from all over the room as, one by one, he gave analyses that were one hundred per cent accurate. He became the centre of a ring of gawping sea-lions, all clapping their flippers and asking for more.

Then he caught my eye. I was drinking my first, and last, 'Tequila Sunrise', I remember. He went very pale and got hold of a chair to stop himself stumbling. There were a few moments of concern, a few pats on the back, and the crowd dispersed. He strolled casually to the bar and asked if I would have a drink. I declined very politely and made a light joke about the effect of the cocktail I was already holding.

"Who are you?" he said, staring into my eyes.

I felt the tentative tip of some mental tendril and I seized it and squeezed it. He gasped and screwed up his face. I did not answer his question.

"You've been sent to take it away, haven't you?"

"Excuse me?" I said, using the American idiom out of courtesy. "Take away what?"

"What?" he echoed, looking at me with a puzzled frown.

"You asked if I were taking something away."

"Taking something away?" He rubbed his brow. "No, no," he muttered in obvious confusion. "Chuck it away!" He pointed at my drink. "That's what I said. Why don't you chuck that filthy stuff away and let me buy you a whisky?"

This is how one trains an immature child.

You may think that I probed that man's mind. I did not. One does not abuse one's gifts. Not even to stop someone else from abusing theirs. I am not a judge. I am not superior to anyone in the world, except those who betray AC. I knew what the man, was doing, of course. I could detect the way he was doing it. He was the one who broke the basic law of magic. You must never use the power to amuse others or for personal gain. Even if they challenge you – one must not be tempted.

---

178. Even the occult titles that they adopt in certain Orders!

"You may not expose God's nakedness just to convince others that there is indeed a God," said Aleister. "Neither should you do anything that would impose your will on theirs. You must believe that the truth can provide its own witness and that there is no need for muscular attempts to convert others. Show the truth – only the truth – and give them time to see it."

The man in question not only lost his ability, he also forgot that he ever had it. He suffered no grief ... but from that day on, he was in no position to cause any, either. That is '*The Law*' at work and I was merely its bailiff. I still am, come to that. Where it is evident that occult wrong is being done, I am required to put matters right. Most of the time I can do this quietly, so that hardly anyone notices.

Security System

Do you remember my 'guardians'? Those astral Rottweilers? The ones like a cross between a miner's leader and an Iraqi General on a bad day? As P.G. Wodehouse might say: they are not too gruntled. They slobber when they scent a public school. They froth when they whiff a convent. As for the O.T.O. – I use Rudolf Steiner to act as a distraction. It's what he was, after all.

These beasts are the opposite of guide-dogs for the blind. I mean, they never walk if they can hurtle. And if they hurtle, they do it like Valkyries on 'Crack'. I did not train them. They came like that. It needs a very special talent to break-in beasts like that. I take my hat off to the poor, armless sod who did it.

Do you remember the man who kept a pet gorilla? "Where does he sleep?" asked a friend. "Where he bloody well wants," came the bitter reply. Please, don't ask me about my 'guard-dogs'. Do not be curious. If they show no interest, be glad. But remember: do not throw anything at all. No sticks. And positively no balls. They don't know that you're playing. Before you can say "Jack Robinson", they make a noise like a bouncing elephant, and there you are – snuffled in!

Like 'Old Nick' for The Devil, and 'Jam Tart' for Jesus ... 'Jack Robinson' was a substitute for Jack Ketch. He used to be the public executioner, and was famous for his speed. He could hang, draw and quarter the condemned man before the crowd knew it had happened. That's why the phrase leapt to mind. My old dogs can't half shift. Like streaks of blue lightning, they are. The strange thing is, I never feed them. They fend for themselves.

An American asked if they were 'cute'. I was at a loss. 'Cute' comes pretty low down in my vocabulary. Under other circumstances I would used 'quaint' in its place. But if you ask me if my astral guard-dogs are quaint, I still don't know what to say. There is no adjective that springs immediately to my lips. If you said "are they unique?" I'd be on firmer footing. 'Daunting' would be good. 'Eldritch' gets quite close. To be frank, 'highly laxative' is most apt.

"Do they fetch things?" Yes, but nothing useful. They have brought a police motor-bike, a statue of Oliver Cromwell, concrete posts with cameras on, and the Western door of a Baptist chapel. There are smaller, less exalted things too: bombs, guitars and traffic wardens. I read Clive Barker stories to calm them down.

Quaint? Not really. Cute? Hardly. I'd put them on a par with drop-outs from a Libyan terrorist academy. You know the sort of thing – demented fiends whom not even the cliffs of Dover could stop. They do what they've been trained to do. What is more: they have no sense of humour. Not a flyspeck! As we all know, this is an ominous symptom in man. In Astral Rottweilers it's apocalyptic.

Nowadays, there are so many ways one can be hurt. When the first stamp was printed, for instance, who would ever have thought of letter bombs? When Caesar wrote so proudly about his fun in Gaul, did he know what boredom he would cause to classes of Latin students? I wish that would-be, occult students would be more precise when we make a date to meet. I suggest something like "ten o'clock at Charing Cross". What they mean is: "the first sunny day in October". After scores of broken bookings I realise that young people have no idea how a wrist-watch works. They like to be much more rounded. When the Moon is in the Seventh House, and Jupiter aligns with Mars. When the shadow of Nelson's column points toward a number seven bus.

One has to be so very patient with them. I am tired of waiting for occult students who are stoned out of their minds. It is hard, you know. It is not easy. Could *you* whistle 'Thus Spake Zarathustra' after standing for two hours, fifty yards from a gentlemen's toilet ... with all that that entails!

All you like sheep
The Churches, the followers of Christ, assume you are attacking
them when you expose a weakness in their doctrine. Either they
are very sensitive, or else they know that their theology does not
hold water. With such a huge drop in membership, they have to
tread carefully. They dare not let their people hear any theory
which might undermine their own. The Krishna people and the
Moonies are a bitter pill to swallow. Rome could have guessed
that tyranny would not survive the Age of Mass Media. Neither
will sanity.

This is why certain books get banned. In many ways the new
'Catechism'[179] should be banned – or made required reading for
every student of sociology. Almost the twenty-first century, and
the church has decided that reading your horoscope in
newspapers is a sin! There used to be papal astrologers! The
church has just asked Galileo to pardon them. She has told the
millions of Africa how to stop AIDS coming to Europe. Well,
when the burial grounds are full and the churches are empty,
there will be no room for doubt. The sheep are ditching the
shepherd, and the church is going to die.

Masonry was the same idea. They prohibit members from
owning or reading certain books too. Yet Masonry has said it is
not a creed, so its members need not fear being condemned as
heretics. They read the books in secret. It just shows that
Masonry is not rock-solid either. Yes, people low down the social
ladder may be tempted by a leg-up. But it will dawn on them
soon. They can't all be chiefs, and have no Indians. The old order
survives: "It's the rich what gets the gravy; it's the poor what gets
the blame!"

In the late fifties, the Catholics had a good go at making
converts. There were postal lessons and teams of priests in every
diocese. In ten years, they doubled their catch. In the ten years
that followed that, they lost twice as many again. Worse still,
fewer and fewer lads wanted to become priests. Mother Church is
using a wheel-chair. As for the Anglicans – why don't they just
give up? They have been wasting away for decades.

There is an emergency, and the churches don't know what to
do. If it was still legal, she would gladly burn all who disagree

179. Written by the French Bishops and selling like hot-cakes.

167

with her. The Good Shepherd has often proved a bloody butcher. But if they tried to throw you out today, you could go to the World Court. Why don't the women of Ireland try it? The church is living in the past. She trusts God to do what she should have done herself. Is it not time for one, last, big miracle? It looks as if St Malachy was right. The next Pope will be the last.

Would anybody care to hear what my I-Ching says about the O.T.O?

Not Now, Not Here

How strange it must be for angels. They float in through the window, sailing on a golden cloud, and before they can deliver their holy message, Saint Anne[180] mutters "What is it this time?" They must be miffed, you know. As a matter of fact, this could explain the recent fall-off in the number of spirit phenomena. Genuine ones have become very, very rare. But there are experts who'll correct a facial blemish for a fee, and there are tradesmen who can provide a ghost to add dash to a Saturday night seance. You need some awe and wonder? You can get it, at a price, but no warranty.

AC told me that he once received a very formal letter, which summoned him to meet God at 3.15 p.m., under the clock at Waterloo Station.

"Did you go?" I asked with bated breath.

"If it had been Euston, I might have done," he replied. "As it was, I chose not to manifest myself."

"Why on earth not?" I asked in surprise.

"Because he forbore to mention which God!" He brushed some crumbs off the revers of his frock coat. "I should have looked such a fool, prostrating myself in front of the wrong one."

---

180. The supposed mother of the Virgin Mary.